What peo

This book makes a bold and
leaders who experience brok
ticipants in God's redemptive trajectory. ᴗ_ _   ıl
stories of wounded biblical leaders, and case studies of Cıᴜₒᵤₐn
ministers, Glenn C. Taylor uses his biblical, theological, psychological, and pastoral experience to address this important subject.
It will benefit all who are called to leadership, as well as church
boards, and denominational and non-profit overseers.

—Dr. Rod Wilson
Former President, Regent College
Vancouver, B.C.

Sometime a person gets sifted and shaped in places you would
never imagine and by people you would never expect, like my
friend and mentor Glenn C. Taylor. I did not know then what I
would learn over many years—that Glenn was a healer of souls—
one entrusted with the "cure of souls."

—Pastor David Johnson

Some books should be tasted; some should be savoured; a few
should be devoured and digested well. Glenn C. Taylor's *Fruitful
Boughs Broken* fits the final category. Writing from a lifetime of
scholarly reflection and practical experience, Glenn seeks to address church and pastoral leadership concerning the terrible tragedy of failure in ministry. He urges those who encounter these
situations to seek full understanding, examining the specific contributing factors in the person's journey that led toward failure,
and then to help that person embrace a wholistic approach toward
recovery in all relationships. Glenn includes several tools he has
used to assist in this process which all leaders will find helpful. I

highly recommend this book for both preventative and redemptive purposes in one's life and ministry.

—Marvin Brubacher
Executive Director, MentorLink
Canada

This book provides a wealth of insight into the complex factors that contribute to the fall of pastors whom he calls broken boughs. Glenn's insight is the fruit of his many decades of compassionately walking alongside pastors who have sadly fallen. His approach is unique in how he draws from many disciplines (biblical, theological and psychological). His study is enhanced by analyses of case studies drawn from Scripture as well as from his extensive counselling practice. Here is a very helpful book for pastors who desire to stay on course and also for those who want to recover from their fall. Furthermore, it is valuable for church boards, denominational leaders and those training pastors.

—Dr. Grant Gordon
Retired Transitional Pastor, Educator, and Consultant

There are many nugget thoughts that you have brought to the surface for us to recognize and reflect upon in terms of personal perspectives and practices. The process you describe here speaks to the need to listen and understand before any truth telling is to be done... A wonderful analysis of the beauty and dangers of success. What it does to us both positively and negatively. Once again, you have presented us with the appetizer that needs to be more fully explored, understood, and practiced... God manifests Himself through flawed individuals... Each was refined through their failure.

—Ken Jolley
Veteran Missionary, Theological Instructor, and Mentor

I celebrate this contribution to an essential toolbox written by Glenn, of pastoral oversight, with a pastor's heart... And, I hope that men and women in ministry can help raise up fallen soldiers instead of burying them alive.

—James Tughan
Canadian Artist, Author, Poet
and President of Semaphore Fellowship

So often when we hear of "moral failure" in the church or in missions, we wonder what happened and respond with a shake of the head and dismissal of the fallen one as weak and deceitful. This is often the response of those in positions of authority as well. Rapid decisions focused on damage control lead to terminating the person without any plan to understand what led to the sexual sin or provide an avenue for healing. The pain and shame resulting from this process may block redemptive outcomes for all impacted. As Glenn says, "*There is no justice in overlooking the overt sin, but neither is there justice in overlooking the contributing causes.*"

Glenn Taylor picks up the pieces of shattered lives and walks us through a journey of reading the many stories of God's beloved; stories full of fruitfulness, brokenness, forgiveness, and redemption. I'm grateful to Glenn for writing about this as I have seen many fruitful servants who "fall" into sexual sin and then are wounded deeply by the response of the church. Glenn helps us look deeper so we can see what might contribute to sexual sin and how many of us are complicit in setting the stage for temptation and ignoring the early warning signs.

Glenn's book is both deep in theology and understanding but also provides practical tools for prevention, early recognition, intervention, and redemptive response. If every church member read this book, I suspect we would all experience grace in more profound ways.

—Karen Carr, Ph.D.
Missionary Trainer and Counselor with Barnabas International
Co-Founder of Mobile Member Care Team
Co-Author of *Trauma and Resilience*

Fruitful Boughs Broken

Fruitful Boughs Broken

Pastors in Faithfulness, Failure, and Forgiveness

Glenn C. Taylor

FRUITFUL BOUGHS BROKEN
Copyright © 2019 by Glenn C. Taylor

Cover Image (used with permission from the artist): LAZARUS - Chalk Pastel by James Tughan, (36" x 36"), 1977.

The views and opinions expressed in this publication belong solely to the author, and do not reflect those of Word Alive Press or any of its employees.

Print ISBN: 978-1-4866-1847-7

Word Alive Press
119 De Baets Street, Winnipeg, MB R2J 3R9
www.wordalivepress.ca

WORD ALIVE
—P R E S S—

Cataloguing in Publication may be obtained through Library and Archives Canada

To those pastors, missionaries and their families
who, being wounded in battle,
courageously explored those dark places
to find the light of God's grace
in healing.

CONTENTS

PREFACE

Pastor Bill kissed his wife, shouted a quick "goodbye" to the kids, slid into his car and headed to the church for an elders' meeting. He had set the agenda with enthusiasm and had great plans for both increasing outreach and moving the church forward.

As he turned into the parking lot, he noticed the elders' cars already there. The lights in the boardroom were on. Very unusual. Normally he was the first to arrive and unlock the doors. The others straggled in just in time or a few minutes late. Briefcase in hand, he shrugged and headed inside.

As Bill opened the door to the boardroom and saw the others settled and in place, he sensed a different atmosphere than usual. A somber spirit seemed to hover when he moved toward his chair. All eyes focused on him in a way that made him quite uncomfortable.

Chairman George dropped the bomb. "Bill, we have been meeting for an hour. We have been told of your involvement with Alice. We'd like to hear it from you, though. What do you have to say?"

Bill's shoulders slumped, his mind spun, and his pulse raced as be processed this candid confrontation. He felt like a guillotine was about to drop on him. Many emotions swirled in confusion as he eased into his seat at the head of the table. He felt broken, naked, exposed, accused. But he couldn't bring himself to lie. He stammered a few unintelligible words and waited for their reactions.

George interrupted his scrambled thoughts. "If you wish to go home and discuss this with your wife, feel free to do so. In the meantime, I'm afraid we must request your resignation. We can talk about the details later when you have had time to sort things out. We are very sorry, but we do not believe you can continue to pastor this flock right now."

Bill scraped his chair back, turned, and walked into the black hole that was his future. Overwhelmed, shamed, not understood and alone, he shook with terror at the thought of going home to face who knew what. He leaned over the steering wheel and sobbed uncontrollably.

* * *

One day, while driving in his car, *Pastor William* heard the radio news anchor excitedly tell of a tragic occurrence in a nearby village. A home had been set afire, apparently deliberately. Two children had lost their lives in the flames. No details. No names.

William's heart raced. He knew many of the villagers through his community service projects, even though none went to his church in the city. As he drove, he prayed for the family and the tightly-knit community.

Two days passed before the local news shared more details about the tragedy. It involved a family William slightly knew. His immediate impulse was to visit them, despite the fact he had miss seeing his child play in yet another high school game Nancy, his wife, lashed out when he told her. "Don't the people in your congregation take up enough of your time?" She never understood his calling to help others.

His first meeting with the parents, Donna and Joe, was a tearful one. They were beside themselves with grief. They blamed themselves for having left the children in the care of an elderly relative while they were on a late-night date. A youth in the town, whom they had befriended, had come to the house to ask a favor.

He had been turned away by the baby sitter. In anger, not knowing who was in the house, he had torched it.

Donna, the mother, blamed her husband, Joe, for befriending the handicapped youth. William offered counsel and care, which they gratefully accepted. He spent much time with them, but their different handling of grief became an insurmountable obstacle and six months later Joe moved out. Donna's faith was shaky and William continued to nurture her through her grief. It was not long before Donna began to confuse William's pastoral care with a tenderness and love she had always wanted. As she became aware of her feelings, she was frightened but wanted so badly the comfort she was receiving. It was not long before William became confused. He began to think that her love was for him rather than for the comfort and care he provided. They fell into sin, seeing one another surreptitiously. Deceit became a pattern. Guilt clouded their relationship but the comfort they experienced in each other surrounded them in a fog of illusion. Unacknowledged needs, submerged under appropriate concerns, surfaced to take precedence.

A few months later, William was confronted by the elders' board with rumors of his inappropriate behavior. They had what they claimed was proof. Two elders had seen William and Donna together. Devastated, overwhelmed with guilt, and shamed irreparably, William, after a futile reaction, admitted his involvement. He was verbally defrocked and emotionally battered, without mercy, by some of the elders. He was required to sign papers which blurred so much through his unshed tears, he couldn't read them. The severance was adequate but not generous. He was asked to move out of his office, leaving the board to explain the reason to the church.

Unceremoniously sacked, William went home to deal with an angry wife and a rejecting young-adult child. He'd never felt so alone, misunderstood, and helpless.

* * *

These are stories of fruitful boughs broken by moral failure. Even though it can be replicated many times each month in North America, the destination of failure as the terminal point of ministry is never planned or anticipated!

Moral failure, however, doesn't always trigger the confrontation. Sometimes, it sneaks up subtly through conflict, relational tensions, failure in leadership, congregational sin, spousal or family tensions, or a multitude of other issues.

This book is an attempt to grapple with this reality of ministerial failure in Christian churches. Surprisingly, this is not a twenty-first century phenomenon. Historically, failure has been always present in churches. The concern for us today is how we handle it in our congregations and minister to the broken and hurt people involved including the pastor.

This book explores the issues that plagues so many churches? Are there ways we could intervene early? Are there ways to understand the process with the compassion and grace with which Jesus would approach the brokenness of man?

You are invited to explore these questions with a mind that seeks God's perspective.

ACKNOWLEDGEMENTS

When one has lived a long life, he accumulates an indebtedness to multitudes of people who have touched his live. Acknowledging the significant input of others in one's life is a major task. I am deeply indebted to many.

Perhaps, most of all, to those who, in seeking to serve God faithfully and fruitfully, have become overwhelmed and challenged beyond their capacity. Thankfully, many did address their experience with vulnerability and came to repentance and confession. In doing so, they invited me into their lives to journey with them toward healing. In this, they honoured me. I acknowledge their courage, confidence in God and willingness to walk, often in darkness, toward the light of God's grace. They remain anonymous but precious people.

Many others, representing a wide mix of professional expertise, have also shared with me their input. Because of my training and experience in theological education, psychiatric institutions, corrections, inner-city ministry, medical services, and clinical psychology, those who have influenced me have come from all of these disciplines. Also, many years of engagement with international missions has impacted my life. In acknowledging these contributions and influences, I will simply list them by groups.

From medicine, psychology and psychiatry, there were competent individuals such as: Ken Gamble, Jarrett Richardson, Rod Wilson, John Powell, Nancy Duvall, and David Wickstrom.

From theological perspectives: Morley Hall, W. Gordon Brown, Samuel Mikolaski, Marvin Brubacher, William Webb, Don Perkins and Henri Nouwen.

In the interest of confidentiality, I will not name many denominational leaders who have provided very helpful interaction and consultation.

Many of those mentioned crossed the barriers of distinct disciplines to encourage integrative thinking and understanding. They have insisted on addressing the whole person in the complexity that involves. The great blessing of my life is to have been nurtured by men and women of such calibre.

Journeying through over sixty years has been my helpmate, Mary, who has never ceased in her affirmation and encouragement. I benefit from the input of two very wise and insightful children who never hesitate to set Dad straight or, attempt to do so.

My writing has been greatly enhanced by the editorial work of Julie Cosgrove who serves a large constituency through the wonder of electronic media. Her editing skills have made my writing much more readable.

My life has been an adventure in God's grace and fulfillment in many opportunities. In this book, I have tried to avoid the complexity and cumbersome acknowledgement of gender issues. In most cases, I could use he/she, etc. but have chosen to assume that these pronouns may refer to either gender.

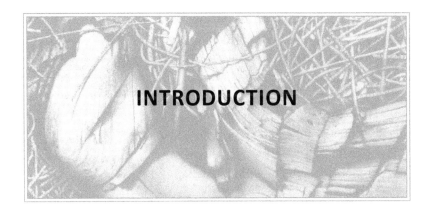

INTRODUCTION

I have chosen the analogy of a broken tree bough in this book for a reason. Fruitfulness is a key theme in Scripture. In the Garden of Eden, all fruit but one was to be enjoyed. Later, God instructed Moses about his laws[1] with great care. In his instruction, he commands that when they enter the Promised Land they are to "*plant all kinds of trees for food*"[2] but the fruit is not to be eaten until the fifth year. In the fourth year, "*the fruit of the tree, is the Lords; it is holy to the Lord.*"[3] A tithe of the fruit belonged to the Lord. Fruit trees were to be protected.

In Psalm 1, the man who walks with God is described. "*He will be like a tree planted by streams of water, which yields its fruit in season and its leaf does not wither. And in whatsoever he does, he prospers.*" This is reiterated in Jeremiah, "*Blessed is the man who trusts in the Lord...For he will be like a tree planted by the water, that extends its roots by the stream and will not fear when heat comes; but its leaves will be green, and it will not be anxious in a year of drought, nor cease to yield fruit.*"[4] The trees are pictured as clapping their hands in praise of God. Jesus uses the analogy to discuss the fruit of man.[5]

I would like to build on that analogy. We will think of men and women called to the ministry of serving God as trees which he has planted. Let's view the heroes of the faith mentioned in Hebrews 11 as trees bearing the fruit of faith, nourished by their exemplary relationship with God.

It can prove profitable to consider the expressions of faith displayed by each of those mentioned. Their manifestation of faith varied from one to the other but together they provide a challenging list. A quick list would include:

- looking beyond the visible,
- being a witness to future generations,
- pleasing God,
- becoming heirs of righteousness,
- obedience,
- placing expectations in God,
- looking beyond this life to an eternal one,
- confidence in sacrificing what was of value to them,
- a future focus; choosing to obey God rather than man,
- choosing to associate with God's people,
- persevering,
- and serving out of weaknesses turned to strength.

That is quite a list! The powerful impact of faith generates fruitfulness. Many of the men and women of faith listed in the Scriptures expressed faithfulness, fruitfulness and failure in their lives. If we read their real-life stories, we get a fuller picture. However, they were, as was said of Elijah, *"A human being, even as we are."*[6] It can be dangerous to forget that fact.

My intention is to study their experience of fruitfulness and their experience of failure. God presents an honest and real picture of their lives in Scripture. There is no attempt to present an ideal. These men and women of faith were jars of clay, just as Paul declared us all to be[7], but they had the treasure of faith contained therein. This book honestly looks at the experiences, the culture, and people that contributed to their failure.

Most importantly, I want to study God's response. He did not abandon his chosen, even in their failure. I have chosen just four of the people mentioned. My only reason for limiting my choice to them is that they are illustrative. Other men or women would illustrate equally well. I do not wish to lose my point in an attempt to be exhaustive. Women of faith faced the same challenges both in ministry and leadership.

We will also look at twenty-first century fruitful people who failed. I choose only three pastors (men are chosen because it is mainly male pastors I have worked with) to provide illustrations of three experiences. There are many other reasons for failure. These are chosen as illustrative but are certainly not exhaustive as reasons for failure in ministry. These are individuals with whom I have journeyed, as a pastoral counselor, through the valley of failure and rejection to reconciliation with God. Tragically, many do not experience reconciliation with the churches or organizations in which they served. The stories I share are painful but a reality for many.

We often view our church leaders as towering oaks, rooted deeply in faith and Scripture. Sometimes fruit trees, when inadequately cared for, produce more fruit than the boughs can bear. The strain may break them. There may be many reasons for that.

The point is that often the boughs break. When a fruitful servant breaks—whether morally, relationally or emotionally—the consequences are drastic. How should we respond to these broken boughs? What is our responsibility to them? How does God deal with them? Can we profit from learning from their experience? Are there ways that the breaking could have been avoided?

These are some of the many questions we wish to address. Understanding must precede judgment. If you are open to explore these issues, I encourage you to read on. However, if your mind is already made up, then perhaps you will not benefit from this book's discussion.

chapter one

BIBLICAL FRUITFUL BOUGHS BROKEN

The Stories of Servants of God in Scripture

WHAT FOLLOWS ARE THE STORIES OF FOUR FRUITFUL PEOPLE IN THE Scripture. They are chosen only as representative. There are dozens of others, both men and women, one could choose. They were fruitful boughs as they lived and served God in their day. Each was specifically called. They were called to a relationship of fidelity that involved expectations. God offered faithfulness and expected faithfulness in return. Each was given a task chosen by God. They were enabled by God. We rightly look to them as models of the faith.

To enter their experience, we imaginatively walk with them. The cultures they served in appear different from ours. Of course, each of ours are different, too. We need to try to see through their eyes, seeking harmony with their emotions, feelings and thoughts. This will require a suspension of judgement. If you view them through your ideals, you will not as fully understand their experience. Until we have walked in their shoes, lived their lives, and felt the demands and challenges they experienced, we must be careful with any accusations.

In following the lives of these fruitful individuals, we will have opportunity to exult in the spectacular incidents of their great expressions of faith. We may even wonder at their confidence in God. However, we must keep in mind that they were men (and there were women, too) just like we are. The Scripture does not simply present the high points of their lives but their trials and tests as well. God was present in their victories enabling, guiding them and in their brokenness responding out of his character of love. This teaches us that we, too, can experience him in the same manner.

The Father of Faith Falters

In the catalogue of faith (found in Hebrews 11), Abraham stands head and shoulders above the great cloud of witnesses. Abraham's acclaim is noteworthy.

"By faith Abraham..." These words have echoed down the halls of the centuries. Down through history people have known Abraham as the father of faith, a title well deserved. Proudly, people of faith have claimed him with the words Stephen used, *"Our father Abraham"* The strong prophet Isaiah urged his generation, *"Look to Abraham, your Father."*[8]

God himself, in the powerful message he gave to Isaiah, speaks of the *"descendants of Abraham my friend."*[9] Jehoshaphat, in pleading with God for deliverance, calls upon God to be faithful to *"the descendants of Abraham Thy friend."*[10] James, the brother of Jesus, urges in his epistle for the people to have faith as did Abraham who *"was called God's friend."*[11]

Could there be any more wonderful way to be known than as the father of faith and the friend of God? This friendship with God that directed Abraham's life was a union of faith and actions. It was a covenantal relationship of faith rather than a legal arrangement. In his letter to the faithful, James is clear to point out that the righteousness attributed to Abraham was an outcome of a dynamic faith expressing itself in the day to day actions of life. James says, "his [Abram's] faith and his actions were working together, and his faith was made complete by what he did."[12]

Abraham's story, as depicted in Genesis, chapters 11 through 50, is a familiar one. However, I will briefly summarize some of the highlights in the life of this man of God that show he certainly was a fruitful bough. The goal is to concisely bring to your attention the several experiences of his life that evidence his fruitfulness in faith. In this way, his overwhelmingly bountiful life can provide a role model for each of us.

The Obedience of Faith

Fruitfulness in ministry begins with a call, followed by the response of obedience. The call often is described as involving a "leaving and cleaving," which is the language of the King James Version of the Scripture in Genesis 2:24 to describe the intimacy of the marriage relationship. The call to faith requires a similar commitment of intimacy, but with God. Thus, it is not surprising that God's call to Abraham was *"Go forth...from your country...I will show you."*[13] The leaving, the going, and the openness to being shown the way and the destination, required great faith.

The writer of the book of Hebrews puts it simply, *"By faith Abraham, when called to go...obeyed and went, even though he did not know where he was going."*[14] It is helpful to know more details concerning the circumstances he was asked to leave. There appears to have been two leavings. In Chapter 11, under the leadership of Terah, his father, Abram and others left Ur of the Chaldeans and moved to Haran, where they settled. Then, in Chapter 12, the personal call of Abram to leave the comfort, security and plenty provided by Haran occurred sometime later. Abram and his childless wife obeyed. By doing so, they moved into the unknown of the desert and into a very different existence as nomads. Together with a small group of people, they journeyed toward the hostile land of Canaan. What we know of the Canaanites would suggest they were a people to be feared. The sojourners from Haran probably knew of this as well. Yet they obediently traveled onward.

Abram responded immediately to the call with complete obedience. Thus, Abram provides a model for all who would obey the call of God in the face of great challenges—unknown and known, obvious and hidden, imagined and unimaginable. But he did not go alone.

Stephen, in his sermon on faith in Acts, summarizes Abraham's call and response in this manner. *"The God of glory appeared to our father Abraham…'Leave your country and your people,' God said, 'and go to the land I will show you.'"*[15] Frequently, it is a vision of the God of glory that initiates a call. It was true with Moses, Isaiah, and Paul. Perhaps, there is nothing more persuasive to action than encountering and experiencing God in such a personal way.

Get out, come and I will show you. The command to change, to leave what is familiar, is urgent and demands obedience. It often involves loss, grief, and separation. Isaiah emphasizes this point, *"When he was one I called him."*[16]

Such a call means leaving others and the past to go into an unknown future. This invitation involves a forward movement and new directions into ambiguity. The future is uncertain in details, but certainty lies in the promise of God's words, *"I will show you."*

Scripture reveals that *"The Lord who appeared to him."*[17] God's response to the obedience of faith is his presence! In reaction, Abram built an altar and called upon God. Faith leads to an interactive relationship.

A call, an invitation, and a promise that does not lead to obedience is a dead end. Obedience is the faith response to the personal command, invitation, and assurance of the direction God provides.

The Generosity of Faith

The next chapter, Genesis 13, tells us the story of Abram's faith expressed in his generosity to his nephew, Lot. After a visit to Egypt, Abram went to Bethel where he called upon God in worship. By this time, both his wealth and that of Lot had increased. They lived quit peacefully among the Canaanites and Perizzites. However, the land allotted to them was crowded, and conflict arose between the herdsmen of Abram and Lot. Abram wanted peace, not quarrelling. His solution was to give Lot what he wished which was the best lands, *"the valley of the Jordon…it was well watered."*[18] which appeared the most prosperous. So, Lot agreed and pitched his tents. Immediately, God honored Abram's generosity of faith by pledging to give him the length and breadth of the land for him and his offspring to use. Faith was rewarded.

However, peace did not reign. War broke out in the land of Jordan with multiple kings vying for control. Alliance shifted until one alliance dominated and seized all the prize including Lot and his possessions.

Again, Abram responded with generosity by taking his trained men to battle, defeating the allied kings and rescuing Lot and his possessions. Returning from battle on behalf of others, Abram was met by Melchizedek, the priest of God Most High who blessed Abram. The writer of the book of Hebrews (chapters 5 and 7) has much to say about this king. For my purpose it is enough to see Abram's declaration of faith and confidence in God as he declares to Melchizedek, *"I have sworn to the Lord God Most High, Possessor of heaven and earth."*[19] His faith is totally found in the God whom he worships and in whom he places his confidence.

The Worship of Faith

Faith expresses itself in worship. After the Lord appeared to Abram at Shechem, he went east of Bethel and *"there built an altar to the Lord and called on the name of the Lord."*[20] When he returned there from Egypt again he *"called on the name of the Lord."*[21] This became the habit of Abram's life, repeated often following each renewed promise and victory.[22]

His worship in faith became the reflexive response of his life. His faith enabled him to plead for God's grace toward Sodom and Gomorrah, thus demonstrating the power of faith in God's grace and the strength and freedom he experienced in that relationship. His worship was motivated by the vision of faith which looked beyond the earthly realities of life to the eternal perspective assured by a God from whom neither age nor death could separate. His faith looked with steady vision *"for he was looking forward to the city with foundations, whose architect and builder is God."*[23] What a vision! Worship in faith sees beyond the stuff of life to the realities of a faithful God and things eternal.

The Covenant of Faith

Call leads to obedience. Obedience leads to God's presence. Friendship leads to covenant. The evident maturing of faith in Abram led to an increasing intimacy in his relationship with God. God was the initiator. Abram responded with growing awareness and desire to experience God in all the realities of life. Faithfulness on Abram's part created the context for promise and a covenant from a God who, in grace, initiated the engagement with one he had chosen.

There appears to be a progressive development of the Covenant which evolved from Abram's encounter with Melchizedek to the sign of circumcision. The fulfillment of the Covenant would only be completed in the fullness of God's kingdom in eternity. It began with God's assurance, *"Do not fear, Abram. I am a shield to you."*[24] Earlier the land had been promised. Later, God said, *"All the land that you see, I will give to you and your descendants forever... I will make your descendants like the dust of the earth."*[25] Being childless, Abram could not see how that could be. God assured him that his offspring would be as countless as the stars. God revealed his plan for generations to come. With circumcision added to the Covenant, God gave Abram the new name, Abraham, and extended his offspring to include many nations and declares the Covenant to be everlasting.[26] Sarai's name was also changed to Sarah. Abraham's response to the Covenant was worship. Eventually Isaac was born, and Abraham and Sarah rejoiced in God's fulfilled promise of a son.

There was a progression in Abraham's knowledge of God. In his encounter with Melchizedek, Abram came to know God as *"God Most High, Possessor of heaven and earth."*[27] In the establishment of the Covenant, he refers to God as the Sovereign LORD, and in the institution of circumcision God declares himself to be *"God Almighty."*[28] He later came to know God as *"the Everlasting God"*[29] and *"the Lord Will Provide."*[30] The growth of faith entails growth in the knowledge of God in our experience of life and commitment.

The Sacrifice of Faith

At the height of his maturity in his walk with God, Abraham's faith was tested. Many have wrestled with a concern about the "testing" of Abraham. It helps to understand the distinction that appears consistent in the Scripture between being tempted and being tested. A common word in the Old Testament for testing has the connotation of refining or purifying. The Apostles Paul, Peter, and James discuss this matter adequately.[31] One cannot know the strength of one's faith without the testing of its endurance under stress. As steel is tested to determine its strength, so the endurance of faith is tested by trials.

In Abraham's case, as a bolt out of the blue, came the command of God, *"Take now your son, your only son, whom you love, Isaac, and go to the land of Moriah. Offer him there as a burnt offering."*[32] What a challenge to faith! Only God, who gave his own son, could possibly imagine what that command would mean to Abraham. The New Testament declares, *"Abraham reasoned that God could even raise the dead."*[33]

The story in Genesis does not reveal Abraham's turmoil but only his faith. *"We will worship and will return to you,"*[34] declares Abraham to his servants, indicating that both he and Isaac will return. To his son's question about the lamb, he said, *"God will provide for Himself the lamb for the burnt offering."*[35]

God intervened as he always does in response to the sacrifice of faith. And, Abraham called the place, *"The LORD Will Provide."*[36] The sacrifice of faith led to the further affirmation of God in his promise of blessing to Abraham, *"because you have obeyed My voice."*[37]

The sacrifice of faith issues in the promise and the provision of God in his eternal purposes. It is not much wonder that Abraham is called the Father of Faith as he was certainly a fruitful bough which bore abundantly.

The Growth of Faith

A bird must leave the nest to learn to fly. It must leave the care of parents to learn to find food for itself, to make a home and to create a family that is its own. With all of this comes change, transition, responsibility and testing. The learning process may be traumatic.

To fulfill God's calling, Abraham needed to step out. To become the father of nations and to eventually create a community of faith that spanned generations, nations, and the world, Abraham needed to respond to God's call. He came to a vision that exceeded the limits of time, an eternal perspective. Although moving into an unknown desert, his vision was of a city whose builder and maker was God.

Faith calls us to grow and to learn to trust in the God who has called us out. That growth will take us beyond self, beyond much of lesser value and towards goals only seen with the vision of faith. To achieve such faith requires maturity through testing, challenge, clarification of commitment, and even failure.

Then Abraham Faltered

The idealist, romantic or perfectionist in us would like to conclude Abraham's story with the celebration of faith. However, we cannot do that and still be faithful to the revelation of God. He who knows the heart of man does not fear to tell the whole story.

God abundantly honors faith while acknowledging the heart of man is deceitful. The Scriptures do not present perfect plastic saints. The reality of grace is only fully comprehended in its ability to deal with the fallenness of man. The saints of scripture are just like us. Just as Paul was left with his thorn in the flesh and Moses was left with his impatient anger, so Abraham did not become perfect, even with his great faith. We must look at the faltering faith of Abraham.

Fear Prompts Deceit

We do not know exactly how long Abram was in the Land of Promise before trouble plagued his family. We know Abraham assumed total responsibility to provide for his family as the head. He had come from a land of prosperity and plenty where agriculture provided abundance. He was promised another land beyond the desert, so he built an altar at Bethel, and continued to journey toward the Negev. Then tragedy struck in the form of a famine. It is likely that he had never encountered such a need and certainly not the severity of this famine. Scarcity tempts faith. When rain fails, faith dries up like parched soil. He knew he had to provide for his family and herds, which meant moving on again.

As he approached Egypt,[38] a land more like the Euphrates delta he had left, fear gripped his heart. Doubtless he knew about the Egyptians both in terms of their prosperity, their sensuality and their power as a nation. He felt unsafe and at risk. He panicked. His trust in the God who called and promised had not matured to strength. He concluded to Sarai, *"They will kill me, but they let you alive."*[39] He developed a scheme so that his life would be spared.

How often do circumstances, with which we are unfamiliar, lead us to scheme and fear moves us to deceit? He requested Sarai, a woman of rare beauty, to participate with him in his scheme. *"Please say that you are my sister so that it may go well with me."*[40]

How prone we are to turn to rationalizing, seeking to sort out what the best answer is as we see it, counting on half-truths to free us from the fear that grips our souls and muddles our minds. His ruse worked in that Sarai was taken into Pharaoh's household and Abram received not only his life spared but received sheep, cattle, donkeys and camels. All seemed to be well except that Sarai was in grave danger and, of course, God's plan and intention was in danger of being thwarted by human solutions. God was not consulted.

The Lord had been left out of the equation. Although Abram did not turn to God, God had not forgotten him. God acted in power and grace, even when Abram acted in deceit and fear to the extent of endangering his beloved wife. The Lord struck Pharaoh, not Abram.

So often the sin of the man of faith has severe repercussions for others —both those we love and those with whom we engage sinfully in our fear. Sin invariably has communal implications. Others are affected. Pharaoh, though not totally innocent, was the victim of Abram's lack of faith. We do not know the source of Pharaoh's wisdom that caused him to link his severe diseases with Abram's deceit, but he made the connection. He confronted the father of faith with the truth and expelled him with all his possessions, including his wife, from the land of Egypt.

Abram encountered "famine"[41] and he went to Egypt. This poses a question: What drives us? There are many circumstances that have the potential to confuse clear thinking and cause us to muddle into the murky waters of deceit. Circumstances create panic. Trust vaporizes into deception. When we feel jeopardized or in danger, we will risk much that is important to us. Sometimes being in the presence of power and wealth, such as Abram witnessed in Egypt, rattles our thinking. Fear in the heart weakens the will. Abram, the fruitful bough, was broken by fear and timidity in the face of power and wealth.

Tragically, we must mention another failure of the father of faith. Much later in his life of faith Abraham (his name had been changed after demonstrating his faith) failed again due to fear. This was in his encounter with the powerful king Abimelech. In coming into his territory, Abraham feared for his well-being and declared Sarah to be his sister.[42] He requested that she also report that he was her brother. Again, in grace God intervened. He warned Abimelech in a dream that he should not have taken Sarah into his house as she was married. Abimelech responded: *"In the integrity of my heart and the innocence of my hands I have done this."*[43] God responded, *"I know...I also kept you from sinning against Me."*

Being confronted by the pagan, Abraham explained that Sarah was the daughter of his father but not of his mother and that it was for fear of his life he spoke deceitfully. The integrity of the heathen king put to shame the father of faith. Abraham prayed for Abimelech and God healed him and his family of infertility. God's grace extended to both the heathen king and his chosen, Abraham.

We may learn from Abraham that even strong faith is challenged by fear when dependence upon God is not sought. Nonetheless, God's intervention is grace!

Doubt Prompts Doing It My Way

Sarai became overwhelmed by her inability to conceive.[44] Only those who have faced the issue of infertility can comprehend such overwhelming pain. This is accentuated when there is a strong desire for children or when age or illness reduces the potential for pregnancy to occur, as was the case with Sarai. The personal agony and an unremitting sense of shame plagued her. The ambiguity, uncertainty, sense of helplessness and fear of blame increased the pressure. The hope inspired by the promise of God was dashed by the realities of her and Abraham's life situation. As their age increased their sense of hopelessness expanded proportionately.

Sarai offered a solution that must have been very painful for her. Love and despair wedded, which produced doubt. She conceived a self-made plan. Love violated love. *"So Sarai said to Abram, 'Now behold, the Lord has kept me from having children...go in to my maid; perhaps I shall obtain children through her.'"*[45] The practice appears to have been common in the cultures surrounding them. Maybe she was splitting hairs in rationalizing that the child would still be Abram's son. Did she question that God's promise had specifically included her?

There can be little doubt that this was a painful decision, but at their age, it seemed to her and to Abram as the only hope. This was a sacrifice of love. Infertility tested faith. The reasoning of expediency was convincing. The strength of faith was shattered in the presence of such agony. The tempting made Abram's resistance weak. He had no better solution to their mutual problem.

As with so many human solutions, the outcome quickly became unbearable. As soon as Hagar became pregnant, the tables turned. She despised Sarai. Rivalry raised its serpentine head. Sorrow was over them like ocean waves. Sarai accused Abram of, *"the wrong done me upon you."* In her frustration and anger she further called upon God, *"May the Lord judge between you and me!"*[46]

A gulf opened between Sarai and Abram. The tension thickened into darkness and despair. How often sin separates spouses! Abram yielded to Sarai authority over Hagar. Sarai became harsh ·

11

and abusive, and Hagar ran away with the child Abram had sired, Ishmael. The fruitful relationship of Sarai and Abram became a bramble of difficulty.

Fortunately, the Lord's angel found Hagar and Ishmael dying of hunger and thirst in the desert. He saved them and sent her home with a promise of many descendants. Hagar felt safe and named God's messenger, *"You are a God who sees."*[47]

God did not abandon Hagar. Nor did he abandon Abram, even though Abram, the fruitful bough and the father of faith, had again failed. The failure was as complex as any we may experience. Infertility, loss of hope, human impossibilities, love that sought human solutions, and shame and confusion—all consorted together to bend and break the faith of the man who left all to follow the call of God. We should also note that God also blessed Sarah despite her failures.

And yet, even when the fruitful bough broke, God did not abandon the father of faith. He is remembered and commended throughout scripture among the heroes who placed their faith in God.

The Poet King Falls

The writer to the Hebrews declared that he did not have time to tell about David and many other people of faith. In my study, I cannot overlook him. He is at the center of God's plan. God sought a man after his own heart and David was that man. If Abraham is the father of faith, then, I suggest, David is the model of faith. He was known as the sweet singer of Israel.[48] David's story is so extensive that I can only focus on what is relevant to my purpose.[49] His anointing and appointment to kingship is a story of high drama and significance. Having eliminated all the brothers, David was called from the fields. Samuel was told, *"You shall anoint for me the one I designate...Do not look at his appearance or at the height of his stature...Man looks at the outward appearance, but the Lord looks at the heart."*[50] God saw in David what he wanted. The choice remained a secret for some time, but *"the Spirit of the Lord came mightily upon David from that day forward."*[51]

David became a fruitful bough in God's service. God declared that David's kingdom would never end, nor would God's love of him ever cease. He was central to God's plan. Jesus is referred to primarily as the Son of David[52] and the heir and fulfillment of his kingdom, God's kingdom, to be finalized in glorious completion at Christ's coming to establish a new heaven and earth filled to overflowing with righteousness.[53]

A Person of Great Gifts and Talents
His fruitfulness was manifest in many ways. No one compares to David in the multiplicity of his gifts and abilities. He was an athlete, musician, poet, and a protective shepherd with passion evidencing loyalty. He had administrative skill, military acumen, and he was a visionary. He prompted intense loyalty in those he led. They were prepared to sacrifice their lives for him, and many followed him in rejection and persecution as he was hounded from cave to desert by large armies of a jealous King Saul.

As a youth, he faithfully tended and protected his family's sheep even when he was called to be anointed. Later, he was summoned to artistically lift the depression of King Saul through his soothing music and song. When the Spirit of the Lord left Saul and a harmful spirit tormented him, he descended into the depths of despair. In his depression, anxiety, anger and emotional instability, he called for the healing touch of David's music.

Perhaps, David was the greatest poet ever to have written words to so effectively plumb the depths of the human heart. His poetry expresses the wrestling of the human soul from joyful heights of praise to depths of agony, pain and despair.

For a period, he served both as therapist to Saul and as a shepherd when not needed by Saul. His encounter with Goliath changed that! When Saul and his armies saw Goliath as a giant and ran in fear, David saw him as a trivial nuisance who displayed arrogance against God. He slew Goliath, not with superior strength, but a valiant faith that saw Goliath as no challenge to his God.[54] In his victory, David wanted all to know that there was a most powerful God in Israel.

The Hunted and Hounded

As a warrior, he fought with faith and a strong arm. He excelled in battle and in plan-full strategizing. David became so successful in war that he provoked the jealousy of King Saul.[55] Saul hounded David as one might chase a rabid dog. Saul raged and took his armies in pursuit of David. Even with opportunity to kill Saul, David would not touch the anointed of God.[56] Rather, he chose to remain a fugitive, a wanderer living on hand-outs from others until God deemed, he should rule. In that experience, he plumbed the deepest depths of despair to which the human soul can plunge. He was sustained by his best friend, Jonathan, and they became a model of loyalty and friendship.[57] His faith in God soared, buoyed by both Jonathan's love and God's promised deliverance.

His circumstances became as dark as the caves in which he hid. He was hunted as an animal on the mountains and in valleys of Israel. He fled the malice of Saul day and night. Yet, he declared, *"I waited patiently for the Lord."*[58] He did not take revenge when Saul was placed as an innocent in his hands. He demonstrated loyalty, self-restraint and courage. He insisted on equity among those who fought and those who guarded the home front.[59] He gripped faith though groping in darkness and disillusionment. His total dependence on God is clear whether as singer, fugitive, or warrior.

This doesn't mean David was not frequently severely tested. His despair flared into anger as it did at Nabal, but he was rescued from sin by this man's wise wife.[60]

The King Who Loved God

The time came when God chose to personally, through the prophet Nathan, affirm David in his role as king. Finally, after agonizing years of being hunted and tormented, he acquired the kingdom for which he had been anointed. It is suggested he experienced seventeen years of prosperity, success, victory over all his enemies. He strategically gathered around himself strong men of valor, loyalty, skill and dogged determination.

His passion for God grew into a vision of building a house for God that was worthy of the majesty of the Supreme Lord whom he worshipped. Plans, conceived in love and designed for beauty, were discussed with Nathan.[61] The Ark of Covenant was brought to Jerusalem. David was ecstatic beyond words. The music of trumpets filled the air. Through Nathan, God promised to establish David and his throne forever. His success continued as *"the Lord helped David victory wherever he went."*[62]

David's relationship with the Lord is a model for all generations. No greater testimony can be given a servant of God than that given to David. *"David became greater and greater, for the Lord God of hosts was with him."*[63] Importantly, David acknowledged God. *"For this reason Thou art great, O Lord God: For there is none like Thee, and there is no God besides Thee"*[64]

The King of Faith: A Broken Branch

After a great and successful battle with the Arameans, David relaxed. At the time when kings went out to war, David remained at home. He sent his faithful leader, Joab, to battle. F. B. Meyer describes this as a "fit of indolence"[65] that kept the king at home resting while his soldiers fought. He had always been at the heart of the action. We are left to wonder. Was his decision due to a weariness of war, sadness of soul, or the accumulated stress of so many years of war and wandering to escape the wrath of Saul? We are given no details. Our imaginations wander looking for some explanation. Nothing is said that might excuse his actions.

Scripture does not excuse the sins of saints. The raw passion evoked in David's heart in seeing the bathing Bathsheba is not omitted.[66] He saw her, and he sent for her even though she was another man's wife and he was married as well.

Whether out of deference to the King or motivated by pride prompted by the invitation, Bathsheba participated. The act of betrayal was consummated. Passion prevailed.

Did leisure lead to lust? Leisure may be a time of testing. The saying, "Idle hands find mischief," has been proven many times. In an age permeated with pornography and a highly sexualized culture, it is easy to understand David's sin. His culture was much the same. However, his action was out of character with his faith. He did not follow the faithful forebearer, Job's, path. Job had declared, *"I made a covenant with my eyes; How then could I gaze at a virgin?"*[67]

Yet, there it is in the middle of David's story. His sin is boldly and starkly presented. An arranged murder was the designed cover-up for their deed! It was cold and calculated. But there is no cover adequate to the task of covering sin. The fallout continued for years in the child's death, the sin of David's children, the betrayal of David and the tensions and conflicts that endured. The relational destruction over the rest of David's life was intense.

David's examples show that there is no private sin. We do not exist alone, and we do not sin alone. The compulsion to continue in sin, once the path has been chosen, is powerful. The consequences are unrelenting and pervasive. Others may choose to follow the pattern set by the leadership, especially if leaders are held in high regard.

Confrontation, Confession, Forgiveness and Restoration

God sometimes gives frightening tasks to his servants. Nathan received his commission to confront David over this sin. I expect he went in fear and trembling to David, his king. Skillfully, he aroused David's values and sense of fairness through a story. Indirect, but cleverly, he awakened David's heart to the need for justice and equity through a fictional account. David's sympathies for the underdog is evident. He responded by demanding justice. Nathan declared, *"You are the man!"*[68] Was there ever more clarity in confrontation? His sin was seen in the mirror of his own judgment.

God's accusation was, "Why did you despise the word of the Lord by doing this evil?" Sin against people is sin against God! Despising people is despising God. The hammer fell and David was crushed by conviction.

When defined as a breach of values and of faith in God, David responded, "*I have sinned.*"[69] Acknowledgement and confession were the immediate response. Generations have used his words to express grief and dismay at their inclination and practice of sin. However, confession must not be confused with repentance. Repentance is much deeper and often takes time. One must plumb the depths of one's sin to arrive at a repentant heart. Not only time is required, but also the ministry of God's Spirit and a safe place to explore one's sin in its depth. David's psalms of repentance reach that depth.[70]

These psalms provide words for any who seek repentance in response to the goodness of God. His anguish over his sin was expressed as only a true repentant poet could express himself. He acknowledged his sin against God and eventually also the impact of his sin in relation to others, both friends and enemies.[71] His failure broke his heart with despair. He bore the fruit of repentance in the remainder of his life. He reached out to others in love. He bore the sinfulness of others with grace, knowing himself as a sinner also.

God did not abandon David in his sin. First, he sent Nathan and his word was, "*The Lord has taken away your sin.*"[72] Only God can do that! The Spirit of God, which had filled David at his anointing, awakened his heart and gave him repentance. True and full repentance led to grace in forgiveness and a continuing of his role as king. He did not live a perfect life, as evidence in the prideful census which was rebuked.[73] Nevertheless, God blessed David abundantly in his ongoing role of king because that was His plan. He promised him a son who would fulfill the dream David was unworthy of fulfilling. David collected the resources and designed the glorious house that his son, Solomon, would build for God.

Sin did not set aside the anointing of David. Great as was the stain, much greater was the expunging of the guilt in forgiveness and the grace that filled his life until he died with praise on his lips. No one has penned words more expressive of God's glory. Hear his words to his son, "*As for you, my son Solomon, know the God of your father, and serve Him with whole heart and with a willing mind; for the Lord searches all hearts, and understands every intent of the thoughts. If you seek Him, He will let you find Him…Be strong and courageous, and act; do not fear nor be dismayed, for the Lord God, my God is with you. He will not fail you nor forsake you.*"[74] What an encouragement and acknowledgement of God and his grace.

Yes, David was fruitful branch —called, anointed, gifted, and a full recipient of the grace of God. However, that faithful branch broke under much strain and pressure, and that led to committing a moral sin against God, which had a full of impact on others. Yet, God did not abandon him. He forgave and continued to guide him in a life of devotion which has blessed many to this day.

The Prophet Who Fell in Depression

Elijah is held in high esteem amongst the prophets in Israel. His life was full of drama. He stands tall in the tradition of the prophets who represented God among a rebellious people. He confronted kings and saw miracles as the fire of God fell from heaven to consume armies sent to capture him. He outlived the opposition of both King Ahab and the notorious Jezebel. Ahaziah, Ahab's son, was also confronted by this great prophet.

Most fascinating was his manner of death. His death is dramatically recorded during the time of King Ahaziah. Obediently, Elijah went to the appointed place by the river. He struck the river with his cloak, splitting the waters left and right. Then, he was taken in a whirlwind.

Gone but definitely not forgotten. His return was prophesied by a much later prophet, Malachi, who (declared the words of the Lord, "*I am going to send you Elijah the prophet before the coming of the great and terrible day of the Lord.*"[75]

So, Israel waited and waited and waited—for over 400 more years. Thus, someone like him was anticipated through the centuries until the time of Christ.

Acknowledge in the New Testament

Consistently, in the New Testament, the Apostles conclude that John the Baptist was the fulfillment of that promise. Jesus had said of John, *"If you are willing to accept it, he is Elijah who was to come."*[76] Some of the people thought Jesus might be Elijah. The encounter with Moses and Elijah on the Mount of Transfiguration[77] with Jesus clarified for the disciples any doubt they may have had. James, the brother of Jesus, after encouraging troubled people to pray, praise, anoint, exercise faith, forgive, and confess their sins, gave them hope with a reference to Elijah: *"Elijah was human being, even as we are. He prayed earnestly that it would not rain, and it did not rain on the land for three and a half years. Again, he prayed, and the heavens gave rain, and the earth produced its crops."*[78]

Elijah was a great man of prayer, and a forceful witness to the God of Israel as well as to Jesus at his transfiguration. He was true representative of the Old Testament prophets, strong and faithful.

The Drama of Faith

Elijah's prayer for a cessation of rain should be seen in the context of his dealing with Ahab, the wicked king. During the reign of Ahab, a pinnacle of evil had been reached by Israel. Ahab was the son of Omri, who had split Israel into two parts, then known as Israel in the north and Judah in the south. Ahab reigned for twenty-two years with his wife Jezebel, who was dedicated to the worship of Baal and Ashteroth. Under their leadership, Israel was led into the depths of immorality, idolatry, and unfaithfulness.

Elijah gave the clear and unambiguous commitment of no rain. *"As the Lord, the God of Israel lives, before whom I stand, surely there shall be neither dew nor rain in these years, except by my word."*[79] The gauntlet was down. The battle engaged. This was God's judgement. Famine would ensue.

God then sent Elijah east of Jordan River where he continued to perform miracles. He raised a young son of a widow back to life and provided them an abundance of food during the famine in exchange for his lodging. Neither meal nor oil ran short.

Jezebel was killing off the Lord's prophets except for one hundred of whom Obadiah hid in a cave. After the three and half years, Elijah returned and sent a message through Obadiah to Ahab, requesting a meeting. In fear of his life, Obadiah delivered Elijah's message.

Face to face with Ahab, Elijah presented his challenge for Israel to witness. He called four hundred and fifty prophets of Baal, four hundred of Jezebel's prophets, and all Israel to Mount Carmel. Elijah mocked the false prophets and humiliated their pretensions to represent the gods of Baal.

In dramatic fashion the contest was settled. Fire fell from heaven, consuming Elijah's offering thus vindicating Elijah and identifying Elijah's God as the one true God. His powerful demonstration of faith and confidence in God was witnessed by Israel. As a result, the false prophets were killed in the Kishon Valley. Elijah climb to the top of Carmel and prayed for rain. A heavy rain fell. Ahab rushed off to Jezreel. Then, *"the hand of the Lord was upon Elijah, and he girded up his loins and outran Ahab to Jezreel."*[80] Ahab reported the victory of Elijah and the demonstration of God's power to Jezebel. Her fury blazed, and she threatened to kill Elijah with in twenty-four hours. Elijah's confidence waned, and he fled for his life.[81] It is said, "The fury of a woman knows no bounds."

The Flight of Fear
The breaking of Elijah was initiated by the threat from Jezebel. Fear gripped his heart. He ran for his life all the way to Beersheba in the far southern end of Judah, and who could blame him? Leaving his servant, he went another day's journey into the wilderness. In a state of exhaustion his emotional wilderness began to swallow him. Even the inadequate shade of a broom tree seemed like a refuge. He sat down. He prayed, not for protection,

but for death. His thoughts sunk with his emotions. *"It is enough; O Lord, take my life, for I am not better than my fathers."*[82] In self-depreciating logic and emotional exhaustion, he fell into what appears to be depression-induced sleep.

Only those who have experienced that lonely hole called depression, full of darkness and despair, will comprehend Elijah's state. Suicidal thoughts circle in irrational logic, filling the mind with gloom. The end feels like the only exit worth pursuing. Sleep is a gift but rarely extinguishes the burning pain of misery.

Startled awake by the touch of an angel, he was awakened. He looked around and saw cake baked over hot coals, along with a jar of water. He ate and fell back to sleep. The angel came back a second time, *"Arise and eat, because the journey is too great for you."*[83]

Elijah travelled forty days and forty nights to Horeb. There, the word of the Lord came with a stronger challenge, *"What are you doing here, Elijah?"*[84] He responded with justifying claims of zeal and accusative charges against Israel and their killing of God's prophets. Loneliness and fear had corrupted his memory of Obadiah's claim to have saved one hundred prophets. *"I am the only one left,"* he declared. Personal pessimism projected his own death. Implied is the suggestion that the God who had given him the victory over the prophets of Baal and Jezebel's prophets could not save him from her venom.

Elijah evidences all the typical indicators of stress in his being: physical, emotional, behavioural, attitudinal, and spiritual responses.[85] The main symptoms can include physical fatigue, extreme mood changes, withdrawal, under-eating, emotional distancing, decreased emotional control, feeling trapped, a critical attitude, mistrust, self-condemnation, loss of faith, spiritual crisis, and withdrawal from community, in his case from the fellowship of fellow prophets.

Abandoning faith in God and the abandoning of self are often closely related. The great prophet of Israel was in the depths of despair. The terror of being in such a dismal place is only known by those who have experienced the dark night of the soul.

Redeemed in Grace

God intervened. *"Go forth, and stand on the mountain before the Lord."*[86] God was about to reveal himself. Powerful winds tore the mountain apart, shattering rocks. Earthquakes shook the earth and fire flared. Then, in the gentleness of love in a whisper, God spoke.

The surest answer to Elijah's state was the presence of the Lord. Presence is usually more potent than words in times of grief and despondency. The Lord sent him back the way he came, correcting his assumption of being the lone survivor who claimed to be faithful to God. Indeed, by God's count, seven thousand had not bowed the knee to Baal. God's count exceeded the human effort of Obadiah sevenfold.

Elijah returned to service. Commissioned to anoint Jehu king over Israel, he was back to work. Finding his protégé, Elisha, he threw his cloak around him and Elisha followed. As it turns out, Elijah outlived both Ahab and Jezebel.

In the reign of Ahab's son, Ahaziah, standing in *"a leather belt"* and a *"garment of hair,"* he called down fire which consumed one hundred and fifty false prophets twice.[87] The king commanded Elijah to come down to minister to him. But God's prophet only responded to God's commands. Out of deference to the king's army, rather than destroy them, Elijah appeared before the king. The message he brought, however, was not subservient to the king's wishes. His harsh words against the evil king was from God's command, *"You shall not come down from the bed where you have gone up, but shall surely die."*[88]

Elijah was restored from depression and despair to serve until God had fulfilled in him his purpose and will. Then, and only then, when his work was finished, did God take Elijah to himself. In company of Elisha, Elijah struck the river Jordon, separating the waters, and crossing the river on dry land, he was *"went up by a whirlwind to heaven."*[89] He could not be found by fifty men who searched there for days.

Fallen and restored, Elijah became the one anticipated to precede the coming of the Messiah.[90] Elijah appeared centuries later in discussion with Jesus on the Mount of Transfiguration. He was a fruitful bough which broke in exhaustion and hopelessness—but was restored, healed and served in faith.

Peter: When Certitude Crumbles

The calling of the Twelve Disciples by Jesus is a fascinating story. The first to be called had been attracted to John the Baptist, Jesus' elder cousin. John referred to Jesus as "the Lamb of God."[91] This apparently tweaked the interest of two of the disciples of John. They began to follow Jesus. *"Turning around, Jesus saw them following and asked, 'What do you want?' They said, 'Rabbi' (which means 'Teacher'), 'where are you staying?' 'Come,' he replied, 'and you will see.'"*[92]

What seemed an innocent question, led to Jesus inviting them to follow him. Andrew, one of the two, immediately brought Simon, his brother to Jesus. That was the start of a very interesting interaction between Jesus and Simon, whom he later named Peter.[93] Through this association, we learn much about Peter as he followed Jesus to his death on the cross and beyond.

Peter: the Natural Born Leader

Along with James and John, his partners, Simon Peter followed Jesus. Much mystery surrounds the early disciples and the discernment Jesus had of each of them. However, Peter, without doubt, was front and center as a follower of Jesus. Later Simon came to be known as Peter who would become a fisher of men. Early in Jesus' ministry, Peter's mother-in-law was raised from a bed of illness by Jesus. Jesus felt comfortable using Peter's fishing boat as a preaching platform. When he finished speaking, he told Simon Peter to cast his net. Right away, we get a picture of Simon Peter. He questioned Jesus, but reluctantly obeys. Upon catching a great haul of fish, he then falls at Jesus' knees declaring himself to be a "sinful man." *"Go away from me, Lord!"* he said. Jesus responds, *"Don't be afraid; from now on you will fish for people."*[94]

Peter has always fascinated me. I would like so much to understand more of his life, his thoughts, his reasoning and the processes of his reactions. Maybe, it is that I see myself as so different, but, in some ways, much the same. I wonder about his experience growing up in his family, the dynamics of his business relationships as a fisherman, and his relationships as a husband and father, if he had children. Before going further, I will share a couple of assumptions. It is my expectation that the story of Peter in the Gospels is somewhat representative of similar stories that could be shared concerning each of the other Apostles. Peter, obviously, given his personality, took a leadership role. However, the experience of each of the other followers of Jesus would be equally interesting, for different reasons. It would be fascinating to have more details of their responses, reactions, and thoughts as they walked with Jesus. However, Peter stood out, and for that reason, we know more about him. My guess is that he is representative of the others. We hear Jesus' prophetic promise, *"I will send you out to fish for people."*[95] What does that mean to him? Perhaps, Jesus saw the leadership potential or was inspiring the inner desires he perceived in Peter.

Peter: Impetuous and Assertive
Did Simon Peter want the role of "stage manager" at this time? Jesus healed his mother-in-law of a fever. The following morning, Jesus sought a solitary place for prayer. He interrupts Jesus' prayer time by saying, *"Everyone is looking for you."*[96]. Similarly, on the Mount of Transfiguration, Peter impulsively offers his suggestion of building three tabernacles. His recommendation is deflected by God's declaration, *"This is my son, whom I have chosen; listen to him!"*[97]

It was Peter who challenged Jesus to invite him to walk on the water.[98] It was Peter who declared that although everyone else would deny him, he would be willing to die with him. When Jesus asked the disciples, *"Who do you say that I am?"* Peter responded with the immediate confession, *"You are the Christ!"*[99] Again, at the Last Supper, Peter refuses to have Jesus wash his feet but, when Jesus responds that it is necessary, he recants with the desire for an entire bath.[100] He appears to jump in with ready responses, challenges or proposals. He seemed too often express himself before

24

giving much thought to what he was saying. Almost every time he impetuously reacts, Jesus deflects his suggestion.

Peter: Under Pressure Falters

These declarations about Peter's response were not just impulsive or impetuous but, I think, expressive of his commitment and desire to be faithful. However, his certitude faltered. In the Garden of Gethsemane, at Jesus' greatest time of need, Peter fell asleep, along with the others.[101] I dare say that the emotional exhaustion arising from what happened at the Last Supper played a role. Confusion stretched his credence as Jesus talked of betrayal, loyalty, the need for cleansing, and the anticipation of death. How could these things be? Jesus had challenged his loyalty by telling him, *"Simon, Simon, Satan has asked to sift you all as wheat. But I have prayed for you, Simon, that your faith may not fail. And when you have turned back, strengthen your brothers."*[102]

In the Garden, Peter, along with the other two who had been selected to be with Jesus as he prayed, fell asleep. Again, Jesus confronted them saying, *"Why are you sleeping?"*[103] Into the deep darkness of the Garden, the rabble came to arrest Jesus. Peter, characteristically, pulls his sword to defend his master. Again, Peter was rebuked by Jesus's command, *"No more of this!"*[104] With dark words, Jesus confronts the chief priests, *"This is your hour - when darkness reigns."*[105] They led him away. The disciples evaporated into the darkness, just as Jesus had said.

Peter followed at a distance. John appears to have had some 'inside' contacts and arranged for Peter to be let into the courtyard where the mock trial was to begin. Can you enter Peter's experience in these few hours? He'd been challenged, bewildered, confused, disoriented, overwhelmed by the hour of darkness, and rejected in his attempt at defense! But at this moment while his Lord is on trial Peter is lonely among belligerent, armed soldiers and fearful of life itself! Is this what Satan's sifting was all about? Desperately experiencing not only the dark, cold night but what others have named the dark night of the soul, Peter's certainty crumbled. The fire of his love was deluged with the waters of despair and disillusionment. Wasn't this the Christ?

In fear and anguish, Peter denied knowing him. And, as all four Gospels portray, the rooster crowed, just as Jesus predicted! The floor of his faith gave way and he plunged into doubt. Doubt about the Christ was matched by self-doubt. Bravado was gone. Convulsive crying tore his heart and the tears burned down his cheeks whetting his beard and torturing his soul. Why did not this one who raised the dead, quieted the waters, confronted the Pharisees, and fed the hungry accept this abuse?

Peter's denial was not just another impetuous act. It was the outcome of accumulated confusion, frustration, and anger. Many factors led to the apex of this moment.

His denial stands as a witness to the weakness in all of us. Only the most disillusioned would deny the likelihood of a similar response. The arrogance of bravado or the pretense of perfection cannot rescue us from the awareness that Peter represents each one of us well. The sifting of Satan was relentless. (In another chapter, I will explore the subtlety of Satan.)

Only the effective prayer of Jesus can forestall utter despair in the desperation of an experience like Peter's. Entering, to whatever degree we are capable, the understanding of Peter's experience should forestall our judgement of him.

Peter: Confronted, Forgiven, and Restored

John, the beloved disciple, rescues us from being left with an unfinished story of Peter. He records, to our everlasting gratitude, the story of Jesus' personal encounter with Peter by the shore of Galilee.[106] After Jesus' crucifixion, Peter had retreated into his comfortable role of a fisherman. Having prepared breakfast, the risen Jesus invited the fishermen to take another step toward becoming fishers of men. Personally, he met in quiet assurance with Peter in order to lead him from the dark tunnel of denial and self-doubt into the light of his love. He commissioned him to move beyond the guilt of denial into the grace of discipleship for the remainder

26

of his life. Jesus not only prayed for Peter before his disgrace but came to him with grace in commissioning him to fulfill his role in strengthening his brothers. Note carefully that Jesus had no interest in exploring the 'sifting' experience or the denial but only in affirming Peter's love of him. Jesus pushed Peter to clarify his commitment. He, secondly, required Peter to focus on his call rather than focusing on the call of John. Earlier Jesus had confronted decisively the disciples' distraction in comparing themselves to each other and wondering about who was the greatest it appears. After this second confrontation, Peter learned that lesson well. In the rest of the New Testament, we do not see competing Apostles, even though immature believers encouraged comparison.[107]

Peter's commitment was brought into focus by Christ's personal and redemptive response to his denial. Restored and refreshed, being cleansed by the love and forgiveness of Christ, Peter used his boldness in effective witness. Tradition tells us that he fulfilled his calling and proved by his crucifixion upside down, the prediction that he would die a martyr for Christ.

Reflecting on the Biblical Stories

We have surveyed the stories of Abraham, David, Elijah and Peter. The focus aimed to look at some of the incidents of their brokenness during their fruitfulness. This is only part of the story of their lives.

We must be careful not to measure a person life or impact simply in terms of the failures that they experienced. On the other hand, if we focus only on their fruitfulness or faithfulness, they cease to be examples or models of real life. The sovereign God has chosen to accomplish his purposes and his message to the world through flawed individuals. Paul use the descriptive term, jars of clay.[108] Every servant of God has evidenced sin or brokenness. Obviously, some much more than others and some with sin deemed more destructive and impactful. God has chosen to work through less than perfect individuals in his grace.

Over many years of professional counselling with pastors and others in ministry, there has been one question people often ask. That question has come from two sources. First, it is a common question on the lips of those impacted by the failure of people in ministry. They ask, "Why would you do such a thing?" Or, "How could you as a man of God fall to that depth?" Secondly, the question has been raised by many who have sinned, "Why would I do that?" Many who have come for counselling readily acknowledge they do not understand their own behaviour. It makes no more sense to them than it does to anyone else. They are perplexed, in looking back, to understand why and are exasperated because they have no answer.

In introducing these stories, I asked you to imaginatively put yourself in the shoes of these men of the Bible. I don't know how well you have been able to do that. I want to share with you some of my wonderings about what may have motivated each of these four individuals. In some measure, my thinking has been shaped by having explored with many fruitful but broken boughs the answer to their question concerning the "why" of their behaviour.

Many times, we have discovered significant answers as we have opened our hearts to examining the process that led to failure. When we seek the guidance of the Spirit of God, we walk by faith in a dark journey looking for clues that will enable us to find our way back to God through repentance and forgiveness. We are also looking for the potential to learn, which is present in every situation. There is certainly a tentativeness about the answers. As Paul indicates, it is only in the appointed time when the Lord will bring to light what is hidden in darkness and expose the motives of men's hearts that we will know for certain.[109] With appropriate tentativeness, let's explore some possible reasons why these men of faith fell.

The factors contributing to their breaking were different in each case. Frequently, the context plays a major role. Other times, their past expresses itself in times of trial or stress. Coincidentally, other people contribute either negative or positive influences in their lives.

Without doubt, Satan plays a key role in interrupting our service for God in ministry. Maybe we need to remind ourselves again that we are not seeking to judge but rather to understand the experience of these individuals. There should be no consideration of an attempt to justify or explain away sin, but rather to try to comprehend what may have contributed to their choices of behaviour.

Abraham

There were many things unique to Abraham's experience. Being raised and living with his family in Ur, he grew up in the wealth and luxury of the city. It was a place of plenty located in the alluvial delta of the great Euphrates. It was a prosperous and extremely fruitful land with large wheat plantations and date-palm trees in abundance. With sheltered harbours, it became a powerful kingdom. Idolatry was gross, profligate, and sensuous.

Abram, as he was known then, moved with his father, Terah, to Haran, which was quite far to the north and east. Later, he was called by God to move on into even further unknown territory. God called, and he went not knowing his destination. He experienced transition from one culture to another. There many dramatic differences which required adjustment.

In recent years, there has been much research into understanding the experience of crossing cultures. It is invariably traumatic. Entering a new culture or learning to interact with other cultures creates much tension.[110] Abraham was probably seen as an imposter to the nations occupying the land into which he moved. Dealing with the large and unknown groups inhabiting these areas would preoccupy his attention.

His family group was large, as was his herds of livestock. Moving from place to place while living in tents would bring many challenges. Assuring daily provision would become a preoccupation. As he moved down through what is now Palestine, he encountered drought and famine. This was a dramatic change from the agricultural plenty of Ur. Driven by famine, he decided to leave for Egypt. Many have experienced the drive that leads to bad outcomes. There he encountered a very prosperous and powerful nation, not unlike Ur. No doubt he felt greatly outnumbered. He needed food and water. The wealth of Egypt would have been intimidating.

He became fearful for his life. We do not know how he became aware of the reality that Pharaoh would be attracted to his beautiful wife but, with that awareness, Abram developed a deceitful plan. Fearing for his life, he lied. When vulnerable, he tried to cover the truth with the flimsy falsehood of lie. A similar fear overtook him as he encountered another powerful king, Abimelech.

Fear is a great motivator. Rationalization, which permits dealing lies or half-truths, comes readily. Abraham's fear placed his wife in great jeopardy but also, in God's eyes, it endangered both Pharaoh and Abimelech.

We can only guess what motives led Abraham to accept the proposal of Sarah to take her handmaiden as a substitute to give him an heir. We know Abraham and Sarah were both older, beyond child-bearing age. Did a sense of their own inadequacy and the limitation of age lead them to seek an alternative? They longed for the offspring God had promised but lost all hope that they could bear a child.

Infertility invariably creates stress in spousal relationships. Having walked with couples through that experience, I have shared their pain and sense of deficiency, futility and sorrow. This, I have no doubt, played heavily on the mind of both Sarah and Abraham. When things look impossible from our limited perspective, we tend to grab at straws. Also, it would appear the long delay in God fulfilling his promise led to a severe questioning of faith. Without faith, we grasp at self-determined solutions.

David

David's experience was very different. We know quite a bit about David. He was the youngest of many children. His role and life in the family may have been minimized by the older brothers. He was assigned the lowly task of herding sheep while the big boys went off to war. He had great health and was a hearty lad who developed skill, commitment, and a strong faith in God. His unerring faith and commitment to God's will, as he understood it, shines strong. His temperament was that of a musician, poet, and man of words. But he was also a great soldier, leader of men, visionary, and a planner of strategy. He elicited loyalty and friendship.

One wonders about the impact of his years as a fugitive. After years of being dogged by armies, faced with food shortage and deprivation, he became king. The transition from fugitive to king would have been dramatic.

As king, his success in war became legendary. However, at the time of his fall with Bathsheba, he had not gone to war as was the habit of all kings. Maybe he was weary of war. Maybe he was resting on his success. He delegated his responsibility to others. Maybe F.B. Meyer was right in suggesting a "fit of indolence."[111] Whatever his emotional state, David had lost, at least momentarily, his awareness of God. The sensual enticement of visual provocation led to impulsive action. This seems unusual, given his restraint when opportunity to dispose of his would-be killer presented itself. In the situation where he knew his dependence was upon God, his faith had sustained him. He had yielded to the sacrificial decision to let God, in his timing, take care of Saul. But this time, he took his fate in his own hands.

The power of pornography is most potent in times of leisure, aloneness, or stress-induced apathy. David's convictions and faith left him in the face of the fire of lust. Was his kingship a lonely place? Leadership, adulation, and success often appear to lead to vulnerability and the justification of inappropriate action. Sometimes it is the illusion of a felt need that impels us to make rash decisions. Sometimes it is an appropriate need met in unhealthy ways.

There can be little justification for David's cool, calculated decision to do away with the loyal friend he'd betrayed. Which is the greater sin? We have no instruments for measuring the magnitude of sin. We only know that one sin led to another so gross and dishonouring to the faithfulness of a loyal officer that it stuns the mind to disbelief. Passion prevailed. However, an understanding that leads to repentance is the best outcome for us, as it was for David.

Elijah

Elijah went from the mountain top of victory to the desert of defeat. No doubt he was exhausted after the challenge of the conflict with Baal and his servants. The emotional high of such a success is often the path to defeat. Add to the emotional high of victory the physical exhaustion of running to Beersheba and sum becomes overwhelming. The threat of death from Jezebel and another physically draining journey into the wilderness accumulated into death-wishing weariness.

Today, we understand the chemical and physical toll of stress. The body has its limits. The will is wasted to inaction in response to extreme fatigue. Emotional exhaustion, coupled with physical collapse, creates a hurricane of chemical and neurological responses that shuts down both body and mind. Suicidal thoughts are a refuge at such times. Sleep is a retreat from reality, the stupor of forgetfulness a reprieve.

Elijah's energy also diminished due to a lack of sustenance. Hunger weakens the entire physical and emotional systems of the body. Paul, the Apostle, defines this in terms of physical hardships, distresses, sleepless nights, conflicts within and without, pressure as well as the spiritual conflict of struggling with sin.[112] He would have understood Elijah's condition. Alone and desperate, Elijah sank into a depression as deeply as any man has experienced. The payment exacted by prolonged stress is very high.

Peter

To stand in the shoes of Peter is a frightening experience. Follow him during the last few days of the life of Jesus. He expressed high hopes in his desire to be loyal. He had been a spokesman for the disciples in declaring Christ as the Messiah. Yet, in his attempts to lead, he was often rebuked with scalding confrontation. God confronted him on the Mount of Transfiguration and Jesus harshly said, *"Get behind me, Satan."*

At the Last Supper, Peter declared his loyalty to death. It is my assumption that Peter's thinking became increasingly befuddled as he declared his faith but did not comprehend Jesus' prediction of his own death. How could you put together the coming kingdom with the death of the king you anticipated would establish that kingdom? It made no sense to Peter. Whatever did Jesus mean when he said, *"Satan desires to sift you as wheat?"* There, in the Garden, at the arrest, he tried to protect his king by flashing his sword, only to be reprimanded. Then, of all things, Jesus submitted to arrest. He watched while Jesus was abused, helplessly standing by with no way to use his strength or to express his loyalty. Next, Peter was chided and centred out around the fire, while watching Jesus do nothing to defend himself. Hopelessness and despair consumed his mind. To him, everything was going down the drain. What could he do? All the other disciples, excepting John, had dispersed. He was alone in enemy territory. Disillusioned and defeated, he broke. Challenged, he denied the one to whom he had pledged loyalty to the death.

One thing is common to all these stories. God did not abandon Abraham when he sinned. Elijah was comforted and restored by God and informed of God's perspective. David was forgiven and glorified God for many years. Peter was nurtured by Jesus in the expression of his love and commissioned to carry on. They were all fruitful boughs that broke. Many different reasons and many contributing factors are evidenced in each case. Yet, they were all led to repentance where that was appropriate. Then they were healed, restored, and continued in their service to the God of grace. Yes, the consequences of their sins were not removed but their sin was forgiven. None were abandoned.

Breakfast (A poem of James Tughan, 2001: For Peter)

How do you fix something like this?
How do you look your hero in the eye
and take back the words, the shaking
the words that saved your own skin
while his was being flayed
and swept bleeding of the stones
of the garrison courtyard?

How do you prepare for this?
How do you account for your actions
When push come to shove, when fear
paralyzed your senses, your promises,
all your gallant naïve promises
simply mocked by a lousy rooster
with impeccable timing.

How do you wish for sunrise,
replay the news from a breathless Mary
with a full heart, when it would be easier…
so much easier to remain submerged
in the shock of trauma, numbness
and bloodstained sandals worn down
immeasurably thinner on Golgotha?

Why not sit here in the stern, sewing nets
Inhale the familiar and comfortable rhythm
of the Galilee shallows massaging sand and
playing the sheets against the mast
while I stare out at the receding fog
about as welcome an omen as that voice,
that voice calling me from the shore.

Summary:

1. Abraham, Elijah, David and Peter provide examples of fruitful servants who experienced failure and forgiveness.
2. The reasons for failure were different in each case. Fear, frustration, overwhelming opposition, disillusionment, despair and disappointment where some of the emotions experienced physically, relationally and spiritually.
3. Failure is an outcome, rather than a choice.

chapter two

MODERN FRUITFUL BOUGHS BROKEN

THE STORIES I AM ABOUT TO TELL YOU ARE OF MODERN PASTORS WITH whom I have journeyed. Yet, they are remarkably the same as the Biblical stories. Please note I have given them and their families fictitious names. They are also fictional in the sense that they tell no one person's story. They represent the life experience of real people. Thus, their anonymity protects both the innocent and the guilty. There is no attempt to justify anyone's behaviour. I have tried to include the various individuals or groups who played a role in each story without bias or blaming anyone. If we can keep an open mind long enough, we can get a more holistic picture of what contributed to the experience of the individuals. We must try to avoid judgment until we know and understand the contributing factors. Even with the degree of understanding we may achieve, we still are very limited in our objectivity in assessing responsibility.

Maybe I can expand that by sharing a brief perspective on the role of counselling. It was in that context that I became aware of what contributes to the breaking of pastors. My role was to create a safe place where people, who wished to do so, could explore their experience. Safeness is required if vulnerability is to be quieted, anger is to be permitted, openness encouraged, and truthfulness explored. Listening rather than telling is a key.

My role is to provide guidance in the process of exploring one's total experience in order to achieve an understanding of the many facets of experience that came together to create a crisis.

Inhibition and rationalization interfere with exploration. Self-blame or the blame of others must be avoided. Early in the process, these put a nail in the coffin of discovery. The goal is not to assign guilt but to grope through the darkness of accumulated despair to find sources or contributors to the outcome. Sometimes being quiet enough to hear the whispers of truth or the guidance of the Holy Spirit is necessary.

Facing the origins of the dark experiences of life takes courage. Only in the presence of another, with the guidance of the Holy Spirit, will one find the freedom to explore and to discover. There must be present what used to be called "unconditional positive regard." This enables sharing in depth without fear of shame or blame. The modern term, which expands that somewhat, is mindfulness. Mindfulness is essentially accepting into one's awareness, thoughts, emotions, physical sensations, and inclinations with an acceptance to achieve understanding. It is extremely helpful to be able to explore these things in a safe place. From a theological perspective, this is the love that the Scripture teaches. It is necessary to the process of discovery and understanding. It is not the end of the process but the process itself.

We share each other's faith and hope. The unconditionality of love keeps us moving forward. Exploring the unknown can be frightening. For this reason, we must pace ourselves by providing time between exploratory adventures to let the soul finds its way to truth. We seek the guidance of the Holy Spirit.

Similar to panning for gold, filtering the flecks of gold "revelations" from the "gunch" of past experience is slow work. Gold settles as the swirling mixture of water, earth, and ore is swished about. We search for the gold of understanding and the insight to free us from the past, and this teaches us to move forward. When a freedom to openness is achieved, most people will eventually see what their responsibility was more clearly and will understand the multiple contributors to the outcome.

There is much pain in this process. If one seeks the guidance of the Holy Spirit during this discovery, he will receive amazing help. God's perspective provides the only perfect understanding. Our goal is to achieve the degree of understanding that we are capable of, and to maximize learning and clarity to move forward in our lives.

These stories are a compilation of many. My opportunity has permitted me to journey with thousands of people in ministry. The fruitfulness of most has been great cause for celebration. Those fruitful boughs who have broken, often during times of great fruitfulness, are the source for these stories.

Men and women have opened their lives to share their stories. Many have opened the windows of their souls to plumb the depths of painful experiences. To do so, they must learn to recount their experience without judgment. Only after in-depth understanding are they able to accept responsibility for their role in their story and acknowledge the role of others and circumstances beyond their control.

In addition, only after that depth of understanding can true and full repentance or forgiveness be experienced. When people are "found out," they may confess. That confession is rarely more than a sorrow for being caught. True confession will only come when one has explored the origins, development, and progression of the "sin." Then one can truly confess. Only then will the full consequences and impact on their lives, and the lives of all touched by the brokenness, be understood. This is a lengthy process, which usually requires very careful and plan-full guidance.

These stories are about success and failure. Indeed, failure in success. I have shared only a small picture with no attempt to cover the whole spectrum. They are simply illustrations. I confess that in writing these stories, I often wept since they brought back painful memories of people who trusted me enough to let me walk with them through emotionally raw valleys. Many, by God's grace, found their way to healing. Some discovered the path to renewal in fellowship in the community. A few achieved restoration in their ministry. These three elements —healing, renewal in fellowship, and restoration to ministry—are very different and occur over a different time line. More on that later.

Broken by Stress

Pastor Jim's experience is similar to that of Elijah. The "Baal gods" in Jim's congregation were called by different names —growth in numbers, financial security, the largest attendance in the city compared to other churches and the right community influencers in the congregation. However, they were as deeply embedded in the culture as were the gods of Baal in the culture of Israel during Elijah's time. The culture in Jim's Christian community was one of control, competition, and material success. Those on the leadership team of the church spiritualized these goals. They may have been the people Paul had in mind when he wrote of *"those who take pride in what is seen rather than in what is in the heart."*[113] Of course, some who worship these gods aspired to and achieved leadership roles as elders or deacons. They became respected and admired for their influence. They were guardians and carriers of the culture of the church from generation to generation and not above the art of creating family dynasties.

The Subtle Accumulation

The elders pushed for the acquisition of a prominent property in the city. Pastor Jim became the foremost fund raiser, the top negotiator with city politicians and, because he became so well-known, he was expected to be the major social attraction. He simply did his thing. Jim was a gregarious type who loved involvement with people.

His friendliness and willingness to pitch in to any good cause, however, placed great demands on his life. He participated in most of the community events. He cheered loudly at baseball, soccer and other local team games. He became very appreciated in the town. In fact, he became more popular in town than he was in his own church.

The previous pastor had been a scholar, loving privacy and a well-stocked library. Jim didn't meet those expectations. He was a student of people. Jim's sermons were cheerful, positive, and affirming rather than scholarly. They were a bit like "storytelling" with lots of personal application.

The pressure from the top was subtle but powerful. The best secretary was hired to keep his calendar filled with timely and significant appointments. He was the face of the church in the community. The neck that turned that face functioned behind the boardroom doors. His popularity in the community was important. It was only second in importance to his humility and they knew how to keep him humble. That was not hard.

A few members of the Board felt particularly called to the high standards of Christian living as they interpreted them. These board members often questioned his excessive involvement in the community. They wanted no compromise with the world. There were standards of separation that needed to be secured. Jim experienced the sting of their critique. On the other hand, some members of the Board were more concerned about growth than separation. Jim felt the tug from both groups in the Board even though those differences were never overtly acknowledged. When it came to a vote on any issue, it could go either way. The two factions were very real but quite hidden behind a veil of congeniality. The subtlety confused Jim.

The issues of difference among Board members were judiciously hidden in the interest of the larger picture of success and prestige. Jim felt the squeeze but did not know how to address it. He was a bit intimidated by the Board and fearful to raise what he sensed was going on. He had humble beginnings but a large and generous heart. They helped his humility by giving him an inadequate salary and enough pressure to produce by asserting accountability through data measurement and regular assessment of what God was doing in their midst.

It is true, Jim loved the pressure. He thrived on challenges, especially the needs of an enlarging congregation. He spent hours each week nurturing the new believers, weeping with those who wept, and celebrating with those with cause for joy or praise. Love for people and a desire to serve moved him. He was just as excited about his three kids and justly proud of his wife, Sally, and her ability to earn a second salary for the home. They needed that to provide for the kids who grew from toddlers to teens in what seemed no time. The kids took after Dad in activity and engagement. Sports, music lessons, and group activities filled their schedules. Of course, the price for all of that was steep. It not only stretched the budget but the schedule. Jim and Sally had little time alone. Life was too full. They had faith to believe that God would honor their sacrifice and see them through.

Even after the elders hired an associate for Jim, he continued his pastoral care of the congregation. He let his associate focus on youth and music. The church grew and that pleased the leadership. He was loved and appreciated. Like many pastors, he went through the fifteen-year crisis when he wondered if he could keep it up. His energy was lessening. His new associate took some of the pressure off. He, with good humor, pushed on by reaching out to the needy, the sick, the less fortunate, and the hurting people of the city. People turned to him in need and he met them with open arms. About his eighteenth year, weariness set in. He began to experience fatigue and didn't sleep as well at night. Stomach complaints necessitated medical assessment but that was inconclusive. He became moody at times when alone in his office and his mind would wander as he tried to prepare sermons. At these times when concentration failed, he ruminated and began to feel resentful toward the expectations of the "hands on" elders. Their expectations only increased while his vision and energy decreased with his inner turmoil.

He began to feel a coolness in his spiritual devotional times. They had become routine. Maybe he was losing it. He knew he was not measuring up to the expectations of the board. Even at home, though he felt loved, he was not adequately providing. These recurring thoughts circled the circumference of his mind. He could not get a handle on what was the primary problem from which the unrest stemmed. They became mixed and muddled as he regurgitated them. Sally was becoming haggard with expectations from her work as well as with the increasing needs and expectations from the kids. She was always tired and often went to bed early stating she felt exhausted. They didn't have much time together and were usually too tired for the expression of love that had be so important to them earlier in their marriage.

Unless constantly involved in interaction with needy people, he brooded in loneliness. He felt squeezed like an orange. The juice was gone. Only the pulp and rind remained. The more he pondered the situation, a sense of failure increased. How could he be so lonely and yet be so involved with people? Despair over Sally and not being there for the kids escalated to a sense of failure in his personal life. Being physically drained, weary, suffering with stomach discomfort, emotional exhaustion accumulated. He was spiraling out of control emotionally.

Jim began spending more time ruminating, worrying, fussing over sermon preparation and the demands of people. He became more critical of himself than anyone else could be. He knew his heart and felt his ardor cooling. As a distraction, he started exploring the internet. First, he found games that were relaxing, challenging and entertaining. Soon the pop-ups promoting pleasure seeking led to explorations in soft porn. This grew subtly to extent of the pursuit of greater explicit sexual stimulation. He became caught up in the need and the pressure for secrecy and deception. His need for love inverted to self-fulfillment through imagination and masturbation. What started as a slow leak in breaching his values became a constant way to release the pressure he felt. But no one knew. He was still doing his job. He began to emotionally distance himself from Sally but didn't think she noticed. At least, she didn't appear to. Guilt began to gnaw away at the edge of his awareness. Guilt transitioned to anger toward the expectations of the demanding people on his board. At board meetings, his anger surfaced more than ever before. He became sarcastic. He entered a tumultuous time when he felt he could no longer face himself, let alone others.

One night after a raucous board meeting, he went home determined to disclose and confess to Sally. His conclusion was that the only way to avoid public exposure and the censoring of his board was to resign, move away, and close the door to this unmanageable situation. Sally accepted his conclusion but insisted on one condition that was not negotiable. The commitment was that they would seek professional help together. She didn't know what that meant, not knowing anyone who had experience counselling, but it was an ultimatum.

Jim resigned. In shock, the Board tried to persuade him not to do so. They depended on him. He was their connection to the community. Jim, with Sally's backing, held his ground. In fact, it felt good to do so. He never disclosed the real problem. The resignation was interpreted as the Lord's leading. No other explanation was given to the congregation. Jim's rationalization was it would bring too much harm to others who had trusted him. Especially, it would harm the many people in the community who respected him. Buried in the mist of fear of rejection, the truth never surfaced. It was smothered. They gave him a modest farewell at the church, and he was acclaimed in the community. It was over. However, with that chapter closed they hoped for a new beginning.

Exploring Stress

Stress visits every person in a different disguise. It is subtle. It sneaks up quietly without presumption or announcement. It is cumulative, growing from tiny seeds until it eventually takes over the whole garden. If fact, it is much like the tares sown among the wheat in the story Jesus told in Matthew 13. It is difficult to tell them apart until the harm is done. Stress feels good and makes one feel alive, vital, and moving toward accomplishment. The chemical contributions of the body and brain to stress feel good. Adrenaline energizes. Only as it becomes chronic does it begin to introduce the negative outcomes in very hidden ways. The early evidences are not clear. The longer-term consequences become overwhelming. It is such a big topic and so individualistic that we can only touch on it simplistically here. Let's, briefly, look at Jim.

Background Preparation
Pastor Jim came by his compassion, social skills, and work ethic quite naturally. Although a middle child, he took responsibility for his siblings. In fact, in many ways he provided the support his mother needed. Being somewhat frail, she gratefully leaned on Jim. Dad was almost always at work trying to make ends meet through extra hours and odd jobs. In good humor and genuine care, Dad reached out to every neighbor who needed a helping hand. Jim saw his Dad was motivated to express his Christian faith in hard work and responding to the needs of others. He was Jim's model. "Faith without works is dead," Dad told his family repeatedly. "If others are in need, give what you can and just work harder." This worked for Dad and Jim was convinced it would work for him.

Jim's possessed strong gifts in relationships, compassion, communicating from the heart, and a drive to serve God. The darker side of these gifts was experienced by the lack of structure and discipline. His father's model was a major influencer. Jim's care for his mother while growing up was necessitated by his father's actions. Jim learned to express care and compassion.

Social rather than scholarly skills led to less depth in his pulpit ministry. His "big-heartedness" caused others to love him but led to increasing demands. He was not a manager of either people or money. He submitted to the strong personalities of his board. On the one hand they were executive types who expected performance. On the other hand, the legalists wanted people "saved" without the danger of contamination by association. The demands of those who focused on separation from the world and their spiritualization of their perspective confused him. He was caught between a rock and a hard place. He was built for engagement. His awareness of tensions in the Board was largely at a subconscious level. He felt them but could not have defined them. He felt like he was torn between two very different masters. Church growth was more important to both sides than the unity of the congregation. He chose to move with that intention and desire. If fit his personality. Besides, he didn't know how to address that conflict.

Additions of an associate and secretaries required management and team-building that he knew nothing about. He always "took the bull by the horns" and did what needed to be done, usually by himself. The pressure at home did not come only from financial limitations but the demands of several children. He was motivated to provide. Sally's demanding work took its toll on her and, thus, on Jim. Jim needed someone to share in the excitement of his ministry to people in need. Sally couldn't be there for that because of work and family demands.

Jim, following the pattern of his father, focused more on the needs of others than the needs of his children or his wife. They had not been taught to think of ministry as a family affair. It was necessary for Sally to work to make ends meet financially and her training needed fulfillment. The syndrome of the working wife left Jim alone in ministry. The expectation of the children's engagement in many activities, though fulfilling for them, added another dimension of stress. In such a situation, with whom can a pastor share his excitement in seeing God at work? Ministry impacts families.

He was an accident waiting to happen. The accumulating stress became chronic, and more and more handicapping. With the pressure came anger with which he had no means to cope. As guilt joined anger, the chorus began to fill his mind. Self-doubt, physical fatigue, and emotional exhaustion created a perfect storm. Self-fulfillment of his sexual needs through pornography became the path. He knew he was breaching his values and commitments. This furthered his negativity toward self and he projected it through anger and sarcasm toward others, especially the demanding board.

Jim knew that was no excuse for sin, but the subtlety of addiction was something he had never explored nor expected. When the occasional became constant, he felt helpless. Running away seemed the best answer. He had never run from problems in the past. The sense of loss of control simply deepened his self-accusation. He would not have called himself depressed or exhausted. He had no measuring tape that calculated those elements. He felt no one would hear his story with sympathy. The one exception was Sally. He knew she loved him. If he could get her attention, he would be heard.

His honesty required him to confess to Sally. However, his passion to protect others drove him to make excuses for not revealing his problem to anyone else. He just could not let others down. Nor did he have the skills to face the threatening judgment he expected from the board. The more legalistic members of the Board would want to string him up. He was frightened of their response. He was caught between a rock and a hard place. There was no refuge. Sally, in desperation, saw the solution. She could face neither the congregation nor the board. She wanted to protect the children. They saw their dad collapse slowly before their eyes over a couple of years. They just felt it would be better to see their dad relieved of a sort of pressure they had no ability to comprehend. A perfect storm indeed. Wind, rain, lightening, thunder and darkness came all at once. Panic led to a quick decision. There was no place to turn and running seemed the best answer.

There was a lack of sensitivity or understanding of both factions within the board. The wall between the two factions could not be bridged. None really knew how to address the issue with exploration or understanding. Bewildered, they took the easy way out. There was no relationship with the denomination that would open a door to objective input. The Board felt forced in the absence of knowledge to accept Jim's firm decision. They would have to move on and try to find another pastor. They commiserated and hoped for someone who could stick it out for the long haul. There was no awareness that they had contributed to the demise and the brokenness of Jim. They moved on and Jim moved out! Like Peter before him, Jim "went fishing."[114]

47

Broken by Success

Everyone knew Mel. He was gifted. He grew to enjoy being first. First in the family. A born leader, his father observed. There were other siblings, three in fact. But, Mel took charge probably because it was expected of him. If there were things to get done in the family home, they asked Mel and he was happy to take charge. In fact, he was just a happy kid. He did not need to be told twice. He learned quickly and loved to accommodate in any way that pleased Mom and Dad. The other kids in the home followed his robust leadership. It was a happy home.

His dad was an unfulfilled musician and he encouraged Mel to become what he wished he'd had the opportunity to be. Music came naturally to Mel, and by five years of age, he could play the piano reasonably well. He also had a good voice. His sense of humor added to the drama he brought to his singing.

Development of a Leader

Schooling came readily to Mel. He became a leader there as well. He was just a natural-born leader. The church became a special place in his life. The choir became his passion. His good nature, natural musical talent, and humor brought much attention. Being a good-looking kid brought more attention. He readily accepted leadership in the youth program. He grew to love church and the Lord who was worshipped there.

Pastor Jones took an interest in Mel. He soon had him leading the singing in worship and participating in outreach services. He saw in Mel the potential for seminary training and pastoral or even, possibly, in evangelist ministry. Naturally, Mel's success in his secondary education led to an encouragement for him to attend seminary. He excelled in academics, achieved a Master of Divinity degree at a prestigious college, and later completed a Doctor of Ministry degree.

After a brief role as an associate pastor, Mel was called to First Church in a buzzing metropolis. His excellent platform presence was supplemented with organizational skills. He gathered a team, created a vision, and fostered musical and theatrical talent. The result was the church grew. Bursting at the seams, the church decided it was more economical to start other campus churches than to build in the costly center of town. In fifteen years, three campus churches were started. Modern technology facilitated Mel's ministry through state-of-the-art video-audio transmission. Mel received much affirmation and was given credit for the growth and influence of his ministry.

Sometimes, he worried that success and the attention was a bit much, but the elders encouraged him with a slap on the back, cheering him on. At times, Mel wondered if this multiplication of campuses was not a bit like franchise operation. In some ways, like the Israelites of old, the church leadership was looking for a king-leader who in some sense replaced allegiance to God. However, when Mel had to be absent due to business obligations or conventions, the congregation felt just as abandoned by their leader as Israel felt abandoned by Moses when he went to the mountain.[115]

Soon seven associates were under Mel's supervision in four locations. However, as the congregations grew, Mel felt less attached to individual members. He just couldn't be involved in everything. The potential for anonymity in numbers became a reality. There was a limit to how many he could nurture toward maturity in Christ. A sense of detachment crept in. Distance from those he served and loved seeped into his awareness. This brought some confusion as to what really constituted ministry. The attention felt good, at least, most of the time though he experienced moments of disappointment.

Demand Exceeds Potential

He felt the pressure of sermon preparation but, most of all, it was the administration and constant demands of mentoring a frequently changing staff that became stressful. He had hired specialists in children's ministry, youth ministry, elder ministry, chaplaincy, and administration. He remembered no training in team supervision or team dynamics in seminary.

What, in fact, was his responsibility to them? He was a preacher not a nursemaid for developing staff members. The associates' desire for his attention meant constant interruption when he was in his office. The associates all wanted their share of the resources and they wanted his time and input. He felt respected but used. It became uncomfortable on the pedestal they placed him.

His calling was not to be a people manager. His calling was to preach and that was what he was affirmed in doing. Preparation time was getting squeezed out. He always had felt fulfilled in the creative process of bringing together a worship service. Even that was becoming a challenge. The need to be fresh and new each week in programing was demanding. He came to enjoy the technology in all of that, especially in the visioning and planning. It felt modern, relevant. But what had been a pleasure was becoming a chore.

The tension of dividing resources among competing interests became onerous. An elders' board, mostly composed of business executives, demanded much time and accountability as well. Some of them focused on data, reports, accountability, growth, and resource management. As the churches grew, so did their expectations. He felt intimidated by their business model. He was expected to serve on almost every committee. In fact, there were twelve of them by his last count. He thought ministry was about ministering not administering! He felt they saw him as a role to be fulfilled with little personal content in relationships.

Mel began to feel torn in every direction. His wife, Millie, and their three children wanted more dad-time. Tension at home, especially with Millie, intensified. The energy consumed each Sunday in being fresh and provocative in preaching became arduous. Really, he began to feel the kind of loneliness that only those at the top understand. The buck stopped here!

He felt isolated. Everyone demanded. No one seemed to care. He was just expected to deliver. No one asked about him, only what they needed, expected, or anticipated. They wanted his attention, his approval, his inspiration, and leadership. No one seemed to want *him*, personally. His world had narrowed to a function. He knew he was good at what he did, but no one seemed to know what he needed. He wondered if they even cared.

Quickly, things moved ahead. Affirmed by a supportive and excited board, he pushed on. Some superficial analysis indicated additional staff would help. A board committee became almost a permanent fixture in the task of adding special staff to assume the management and development of various programs. It was interpreted as a means of enabling Mel to do what he did best. He was superficially involved in hiring, yet he received the top-notch individuals with passion for their sphere of ministry. Relief was on the horizon!

But it wasn't. Eventually, he had seven "go-getters" who were deeply imbedded in effective ministry. To each, his/her area of ministry was most important. This required Mel to assume a role of coach, manager, administrator, and cheerleader for this team. He was unsure how to do all of that and fulfill all his other ministries. The churches were going places, sometimes faster than one could keep up. Team meetings were needed. Each had big plans for their area. The elders moved subtly from cheering him on to questioning the many new ideas. There was a lot of activity, but, was their quality and accountability adequate? The budget was growing at warp speed, faster than church stewardship. The bottom line became the main focus, like a profit and loss statement.

Descending from the Pedestal

Mel took the situation in hand as he always had. He addressed the issue in budget meetings with his team. Somewhat surprising to him, he found passion exceeded wisdom in the team members who saw little further than their area of individual need. The jostling for resources became a new challenge. A few tense meetings with elders' board resulted in a recommendation for a consultant with human relations expertise. The Chair of the Board knew the right person. Consultant fees were high but worth it. She was smooth, had the right answers it seemed, but was overpowered by the energy of these young professionals. Corporate solutions didn't work for volunteer charitable organizations.

At a follow-up meeting, seeking to follow her direction, Mel lost it. Anger spilled over, scalding good intentions. He had reluctantly told Millie he would have to stay for a meeting that night. Not well received information! He was tired and not well prepared for his presentation on Sunday. The meeting deteriorated into a combative, comparison of ministry needs. It was Jesus' disciples' distraction, and competition, all over again. Who was the greatest? Who would sit at the right hand and the left?

About ten o'clock, Mel had enough. He blew things apart in an explosion of anger which surprised even him. He saw any dedication to excellences as a disloyalty to the group effort. Anyone's compassion for specialized area became merely a concern for personal success. What they considered needs he diminished to wants. Each one's requests for resources he chalked up to the pursuit of pride. Yes, he laid in on the line. His anger reached a level of attack on the members of the team that he could not do without.

When he arrived home, Millie had gone to bed and he crawled behind her into the cold comfort of a refrigerator, a soft, cold bed and a sleepless night ensued. He almost forgot his annual medical the next day until Millie icily reminded him. That news was also bad: cholesterol up, blood pressure elevated, weight demanding more exercise. Medication could help but change was necessary. The doctor left the burden on his shoulders. What to do?

Sitting in his office late one afternoon, it all expressed itself in uncontrolled weeping. He became overwhelmed with feelings he didn't understand. The flood of tears washed his face, but despair gripped his soul. He ought to leave this rat race. But, what else would he do? He had become isolated from other friends in the ministry. Now, he was an ogre to the team he was to lead. He could not see a light in the tunnel, so darkness closed in.

He tried to compose himself when Martha came to check his schedule. He was too tired to cover himself with the deceitful joy with which he usually greeted her. Now, the truth was known beyond himself. It looked ugly. He needed to provide some explanation. He opened the dam slightly, but the back-up burst forth. That was the beginning of being understood by someone. Compassion consoled the pain he felt.

Innocently enough, he began to share his frustration with Martha, his secretary. She understood his busyness, after all, since she made the many appointments. She tried to shield him. She became his listening ear, his comfort, and the one person who seemed to understand. Mutual appreciation increased with the frequency of their sharing. Mel didn't know he was really looking for intimacy until after he had fallen into it. It is hard for an extrovert to appreciate their need for intimacy with so much people involvement. Passion crept insidiously into each of their hearts. Mel broke! You don't need the details. Your imagination can provide that.

Mel went home knowing he had to share his failure with Millie. He sat in the car a long time before going into the house. He faced the terror of confession. Millie responded with tears of anger mixed with grief. Yet, she knew better than anyone the cost of Mel's success. She had suffered silently, internalizing what she had witnessed. She had shielded him, providing a buffer between him and his angry children. The children had been angry, not at the success of their father, but at his absence and abuse of Dad for which they blamed the Board. After hours of pain and weeping, a solution was determined. They would tell the elders, hope for grace, and leave without fuss.

Twenty-five years of success crumbled. The church kept it quiet, but Mel dropped from the scene into the obscurity of rejection and despair. Guilt, remorse, and anger became the fare at home and, eventually, they moved to another province, and into the obscurity of shame.

Exploring Success

Success is an onerous taskmaster. "There is nothing that fails like success."[116] Danger lurks in the crevasses on the mountain of success. The climb is exhilarating, challenging, and fulfilling.

Adrenaline speeds the heart rate, vigor pulses in the veins, the dreams of achievement fill the mind. One presses on. The excitement of serving God with visible results captures one's zeal. The journey in seeing the Spirit of God at work in the lives of people attracted to the Gospel is worth all the toil. Building something for God is the fulfillment of dreams seeded by the stories of God's prophets, preachers and evangelists during one's preparation for ministry. The joy of seeing God building his church, developing a vision, and nurturing a community of faith is exhilarating. The climb is not the problem; that lies elsewhere.

Not that there are no problems in the climb. For in the climb there is stress, anxiety, and weariness. During the journey up the mountain, the seeds of exhaustion and stress accumulate below the horizon of our awareness. The shortness of breath is overcome by brief plateaus of rest here and there. Successful pastors may rest by take a break to go on preaching missions or overseas adventures in mission. Taking a group on a tour of the Holy Land seemed like a great idea and, it was for the participants. But it can be a stressful demand in daily teaching for the pastor. The new experiences in other cities excite the adrenal glands and we feel exhilarated and refreshed. However, this is a temporary illusion. Each time the refreshment lasts for shorter periods. The recovery time is longer. We continue to climb but are never quite sure where the top is. It becomes illusive. It is like the millionaire who was asked, "How much is enough?" He replied, "More!" Yes, the top keeps moving!

To understand the contributors to those who are broken by success, it is necessary to explore the process more deeply. We are not looking for causes to which we can attribute blame. Rather, we are seeking an understanding of a very personal nature. Moving too readily toward blame usually blocks any creative exploration. It is too easy to get stuck wallowing in the mire of guilt. This limits movement. Our horizon is shortened.

Each person's story is different. Each context varies. However, there are common elements. We are not looking for causes so much as for correlations. That is, elements that taken singly may not appear important but when strung on the thread of time over a lengthy period have an accumulative impact.

For example, in Mel's situation what happened in his biological family contributed significantly to his need for approval. His parents were loving and positive in their intent. Their approval became something sought by Mel and this led to an anticipation of being in the forefront and the need of that position in order to feel accepted. Added to the thread were the beads of approval experienced at school, church, youth group, and seminary. By the time Mel reached the pastorate (based on his later understanding) the need for being at the top in order to gain approval was an expectation built into his DNA.

Patterns of behaviour creep into resistant expectations of which we are unaware. Others often unconsciously respond to those expectations and re-enforce them. Intentionality is not at work here as much as is the mystery of synchronicity between people. Rarely do people intend to hurt others through affirmation.

It is understandable to assume Mel's need "to be in front" and his need for affirmation came naturally. These did not arise from pride. That was the way it had always been. At home, school, or play, he naturally rose to the top. Both he and others came to expect it. In reality, others, such as his board, needed him to be successful.

The subtlety of our influence makes it mysterious. Things get distorted. We may not see the dark side of giftedness because we choose to see only the positive. An expectation or a gift may become a need. A gift that becomes a need, driven by personal desire, is rarely a gift of grace but more a personal expectation. That transition is not readily observed. The "pedestal" may not be sought but is imposed by the reactions of others. The need becomes indispensable, and an obsession.

The dark side of Mel's need for attention became apparent in its absence. His pursuit of perfection in delivery was a search for approval. He had no training for management, conflict resolution, or team-building. An extremely costly part of Mel's rise to the top was the loneliness, isolation, loss of intimacy, and the aloneness that came with it. He was loved by the people, but they now seemed far away.

There were other contributing factors. These would be signs to those who had climbed this path. They were challenges to Mel. There was a short period, about ten years in, when he questioned if this was all there was to ministry. What he valued most lost its priority in the demands of the moment. Administration, multiplicity of tasks, and longer times away from home raised doubts as to whether this was the way God intended his life to be. These questions, which were worthy of exploration, got lost in the pressure and business of success. They also led to a disconnect with his spouse and family.

Another dimension of the problem became apparent to Mel as, through the guidance of therapy, he was led to explore his experience from an objective distance. He explored the experiences of the "spotlight" of success. Yes, it became a spotlight experience from Sunday to Sunday. However, the spotlight was a lonely place also. The shadow cast by the spotlight hid the team that was the real reason for success. He sometimes felt like telling the technicians, "Turn up the house lights, I want to see my audience."

Yes, most of his audience was invisible to him in other campus churches as well as the congregation before him. Who was he preaching to anyway? He was preaching into the lights of cameras. Center stage performing becomes a solo performance. The host of others necessary for the production fade into the background. They become invisible as attention is focused on the main attraction whether that is the musicians or the pastor. Maybe the power of the presence of the prophet replaces the Power of God in the eyes of some. They are the ones for whom adulation evolves into exaltation, known as the pedestal effect.

For some the power of preaching is a substitute for the power of Christ-likeness. Their attribution of power may meet needs in them, but it can also subtly confuse the recipient of their attention. Their flattering works do not speak the language of love.

Adulation weakens resistance to lurking pride in lonely souls. Sometimes the pride of performance diminished members of the team and resentment seeps into their hearts.

The power of the highly gifted may have within it the seeds that can germinate into thistles and briars. Jesus spoke of the enemy who sowed tares in the field of wheat to choke out the fruitfulness of the crop.[117] Many members of large congregations may be planted "tares" who can become quite indistinguishable from the wheat. They may be the immature in faith or those whose minds are closed by dogma and never clouded by doubt. Divisions come if the "tares" are pulled up through church discipline. Some of them are, in fact, babes who need strong milk while others are sown by the enemy. The distinction is not easy to discern but the impact is apparent. Jesus recommended waiting until harvest for the separation, but much damage can be done in the meantime.

Yes, it becomes obvious that the congregational members, elder leadership, and team personnel may all contribute to those who are broken by success. Who can judge these complex combinations of contributing factors? Recall, that I said judgement is not our goal. Understanding of as many possibly contributing factors leads to an insight, which is useful for learning and for prevention. As Paul states, *"My conscience is clear, but that does not make me innocent."*[118] He clearly indicates that true judgement will only occur in the Day of Christ when we each will be revealed to ourselves by the truth of God. We will explore some of the learning potential from these observations in a later chapter.

Mel was justly removed and graciously provided with a severance. But he was informed he should not attend the church. He quietly, secretly moved into obscurity. His family moved to another province and found employment in sales. Fortunately, he met a Christian who saw his need and encouraged professional counselling, which is represented in the above understanding. The family members received help and are working their way to a healthy search of life in the secular world. They do not feel abandoned by God but are unsure about the Christian church. Especially, the children, now in their teens and twenties, are questioning the faith and have no interest in the Christian community in which they saw their parents abused. But God is not finished yet!

Broken by Sensitivity

Jordon became a sensitive soul. He grew up in a rural home that was plagued with adversity. His family had struggles meeting their own needs but never failed to respond to the needs of others. When limited work made things difficult, Dad just worked harder. It was better to give than receive. In that context, Jordon's emotional sensitivity to people was honed to a keen edge. He learned to be there for all the hurting souls around him. Compassion was the mother's milk with which he was fed. His parents modelled all that was best in caring for the hurts of others. There was much to draw from the well of their concern. The extended family came to them in response to accidents, financial crisis and every trauma. There was always a hug, and a place to cry and to be comforted. Their farm house became a rallying and stopping place for people with hurts. Mom and Dad cared. Jordon absorbed these qualities and values. His heart was bigger than his body.

Born and Bred for Compassion

In the close-knit community, the nurturing came from every side. Crop failure, hail, or hurricane only drew the community more closely together. It was traumatic for Jordon to go off to college and seminary where he knew no one. However, he returned home often to have his tank filled with love and, of course, mother's cooking, which nurtured him. He excelled in pastoral studies, the humanities, and in the helping sciences. At one point, he wondered about pursuing medicine or social work but opted for theology with a view to Christian counselling in a church context. In his studies in counselling, he gravitated to the more compassionate approaches rather than more behaviourally or chemically oriented therapies. He became involved in an inner-city ministry in a practicum. Justice issues became a passion for him. His values for fairness, responding to the poor and compassion for all, became keenly sharpened and focused.

Personalizing Other's Hurts

On completion of his studies, Jordon was hired by a growing church in a metropolitan area. His role was to be that of an Associate for Family Ministry. Soon he became known as an effective counsellor. His reputation grew as his counselling schedule packed with hurting people. Referrals began coming in from other church pastors. He was invited to serve on the board of an organization committed to the pursuit of justice for the poor and disadvantaged. Evenings filled with meetings and the counselling spilled into week-ends. Then the senior pastor of the church, with which he was associated, complained that people were grumbling about waiting too long for counselling appointments. Demands were pressing from every side. There were not enough hours in the day.

Three years into his ministry, Jordon began to realize this lifestyle was impossible to survive. He had no social life. Confidentiality imprisoned him in self-talk about the many burdens of others he carried. He had no one with whom he could share. No one mentored or monitored him.

Weary with emotional exhaustion, he fell into bed at night to roll and toss. His dreams were filled with the unresolved problems left over from each day's work. He knew how to care for others but had no one to care for him. Overwhelmed by the needs of others and wallowing in unmet personal needs gave rise to cynicism and self-doubt. Personal critique came easier than personal affirmation. Why was the senior pastor always on his back implying, also, that the board was critical? They had no idea the hours he was putting in! Where did one find wisdom for dealing with so many impossible situations? Where was the God of his childhood and youth? Where was the joy his family had experienced in responding to the needs of others?

He found himself reading and re-reading the Lament Psalms. They were his comfort in sadness and despair. He identified so much with the pain that he shared with others that it became his own. Unlike Asaph, he found no sanctuary. He felt like a beast of burden and found no strength in God.[119] Like Asaph, he saw the prosperity of others and the overwhelming despair of his own situation. There was little sense of community within the church. They had little interest in this young visionary. He alone seemed to carry a burden for the pressing needs of those forgotten in the city. They didn't even seem to be aware of the street kids, the bag-ladies, or the alcoholics and homeless. How could people be so blind to what was immediately before their faces? Where was the vision of the church, anyway? Cynicism circled loneliness in the race track within his mind.

Loneliness and Burden-bearing Alone

Having no one else to share with, he talked to himself. His self-talk was usually negative. The increase in volume simply magnified. The pressure to make visits to people rescued from the streets, and to people jailed for vagrancy and petty theft in temporary incarceration, added an additional burden. He began to wonder where God was in all this mess. Jesus responded to hurting people—even the prostitutes and parasites on society—with equanimity. What was the matter with him? Maybe he was not cut out for ministry after all. He wondered, "Maybe I'm going crazy like the people I work with?" Clouds of false guilt confused his mind. Self-doubt ballooned.

He suddenly realized that he was spending a lot on antacid medication with lessening relief. He was adding pounds around his waist, even on a meagre fast food diet. He had neither the knowledge nor time required to prepare healthy meals. The vague viral-like symptoms increased. He began to feel unwell most of the time. Physical problems were compounded by the mental anguish fostered by rejection, overextension, and the expectations that stretched him beyond manageable proportions. The reserves he had built up as a hardworking young person on the farm were depleted in this foreign environment of the inner city.

One day, while ruminating in his office and perusing the news on his laptop, he saw a news item that stopped him cold. One of the street people he had nurtured to a commitment to Christ had been involved in an accident. His heart stopped. Where was God? Ruth had professed faith a few months ago, received some training, and became employed. She had done so well in her new faith and her work that she had been able to rent a small apartment. It was the first one she had ever had.

Jordon leaped into action, rushing to the hospital to which she had been taken by ambulance. He found her quickly. The injuries were serious but not life threatening, but a long recovery was predicted. He prayed with her, assuring her that the church would help with rent to retain her meagre apartment. He read an encouraging Psalm and returned to his office. In consultation with the Senior Pastor about aid, his plan was questioned and referred to a committee to see what could be done. Not a very encouraging prospect, but a ray of hope. That hope was dashed two weeks later with a brief refusal. Disappointed, again!

Later, he assured Ruth her rent would be paid. He only implied that the church was paying but didn't tell her it was from his pocket. She would never know, he rationalized. A few weeks later, Ruth was permitted to return to her apartment but was unable to return to work. Jordon visited her every few days. Ruth's appreciation was a lift to his spirits when all around he only experienced burdens and expectation that seemed impossible. Ruth loved his care but began unconsciously to transfer that love to Jordon personally. He was the embodiment of attention and compassion she had never experienced. The distinction between loving the care received and loving the caregiver became confused. Fantasy infringed on reality. The good feelings aroused by mutual care and respect, muddling both of their hungry souls. At the same time, Jordon began to appreciate the affirmation he was receiving. The soil had been well prepared in both of their lives to accept these deceptive seeds. They fell into a relationship of mutual appreciation and eventually became physically involved.

Exploring Sensitivity

Sensitivity is a close cousin of compassion. There are significant differences between them. There are other words that express our responsiveness to others such as kindness, goodness, or gentleness. These three words are included in what, in Scripture, is referred to as "the fruit of the Spirit."[120] Along with the other words used to define the fruit of the Spirit, they are the ones that we may confuse with sensitivity. Sensitivity is not listed, nor is compassion. The study of that passage would warrant much discussion. Let me summarize. The distinction being drawn in that passage is between the desires that are works of the flesh and the desires and fruit of the Spirit. These are opposing desires. The actions of the flesh are described as works and they are the outcome of desires issued into action.

However, the fruit of the Spirit is different. Fruit is different than works. The fruit of an apple tree is, by the nature of its source, apples. The fruit of the Spirit should evidence itself in the lives of believers as a natural outcome of the indwelling Spirit in the life of the believer. Notice that the word "fruit" is singular indicating that the cluster of fruit has one source and is a unity. The fruit of the Spirit is expressed indiscriminately without self-motives or the expectation of reciprocity. The fruit of the Spirit may be understood as gifts. We must choose to receive them as gifts. They do not come to us as being forced upon us but rather as gifts we choose to receive and express through the enabling of the Holy Spirit. With the enabling of the Spirit, they become manifest in our behaviour toward others. The works of the flesh are diverse and many, often expressing opposing passions. They, too, will manifest in our behaviour.

Let me contrast sensitivity and compassion. Words are often made from combining other words. Companion is associated with other words beginning with "com" ("com" meaning together and "panis" meaning bread, indicating two taking bread together), or company (sharing bread) or compare (sharing similarity).

Compassion is experiencing a harmony of passion or entering into another's feelings with understanding.

Sensitivity has a different focus. It refers specifically to the activation of the senses which activates bodily responses. This includes the activation of the autonomic, vestibular, cardiovascular, and neurological systems of the body. This sounds technical, but the point is that these bodily systems elevate the function of the body, thus leading to action. This is a state of emotional arousal which, if not followed by action, generates anxiety. There is a genetic as well as a learning component in these reactive responses. The learned component is large. They are emotions or feelings that usually have been nurtured. Expressing sensitivity is akin to experiencing what is referred to as a "high." The person feels activated, energized, and ready for action. These feelings may be experienced positively or negatively. We become predisposed to their expression in several ways. Frequently, those who are alive to the feelings of others have grown up in a family where high value was placed on expressiveness and responsiveness to the needs of others. Outward expressiveness and sensitivity may become a personality trait and may be simply of a reflexive behaviour. Many people learn responsiveness to others through the experience of pain in their own lives. Sensitivity when drive by intrinsic needs becomes a serious problem. Undisciplined sensitivity, driven by internal needs, is as cruel a task-master as being driven by needs for success. Driven by internal needs, it is not a fruit of the Spirit but of desires originating within. Without appropriate governance, sensitivity spins out of control. From the view of Scripture, the Holy Spirit is the one we need to be in control.

This was Jordon's experience. I am suggesting that there are several sources from which our temperament, emotional responses, and behaviour spring. Personality, behaviour, and emotional expression have large learning components. Obviously, Jordon's model in his home fostered sensitivity and compassion. These where highly valued. Coupled with his out-going and rather "type A personality," they led to his over-extension in caring. He pushed himself beyond what was reasonable or what his body or mind could bear. His care for others exceeded his care for himself to such a great extent that it was self-defeating.

There is a reason Jesus said, "Love your neighbour as yourself."[121] The relationship between self-love and loving others is important. When the care-giver gives beyond his capacity, the destruction of the care giver is often an outcome. Jordon was essentially wired for sensitivity. It became part of his emotional DNA. He did not experience the modelling that put reasonable boundaries on his identification with hurting people. He just gave and kept giving. He would have described it in terms of Christian love but there was more involved.

In the New Testament, there is a word for passion or desire. This word is generally used in a negative sense as in the desires of the flesh or of our sinful nature.[122] Another word that is stronger expresses emotions of the soul and is translated as "cravings."[123] Another word is used of Christ's ministry, the father of the prodigal, and of the Good Samaritan. It speaks of being "moved with compassion."[124] A phrase used in older versions, "bowels of compassion," refers to strong emotion with physical accompaniment.[125] These several words in the New Testament imply motivation or an intensity of response. Desires or cravings lead to sin. The compassion attributed to Christ and to those sensitive to the needs of others leads to actions of care for the needs of others as in the story of the Good Samaritans. In times of stress, these emotions become confused and can become intertwined. Sensitivity that becomes an expression of one's own needs losses its objectivity and becomes self-serving and consuming.

It is important to acknowledge the gifts of the Spirit. Our problems in life do not frequently arise from them unless we introduce the human dimensions of pride into their expression. The gifts of the Spirit are driven by the work of the Holy Spirit in our lives, rather than from our needs, and are functions that do not lead the giver to distress but to action. This is illustrated by Christ and the Good Samaritan. Sensitivity to others aroused them to action. It was a response determined by the needs they encountered. It was expressed in a willful, rational action that was objectively determined, not in response to their need to be able to respond. This is a key distinction. Responses, drawn by the needs of others and responded to with objectivity, have a much different impact on the giver than those that are a fulfillment of the needs of the giver.

Jordon did not learn that the love of others requires a balance with the love of self. Those who learn to care deeply for others, but do not learn to self-care, rarely endure. The challenge to endurance is stretched beyond limits by the intense, prolonged caring and serving of the needs of others. The term "moved with compassion" as it is used of Jesus, the Good Samaritan, and the father of the prodigal has a physical component in it. It directs us to the inward movement physiologically that we would refer to as gastro-intestinal motility, or, more simply put, a churning stomach. It is more than that because it activates our nervous systems but is controlled by a mindful commitment and careful action that does not consume the giver. However, being in this state constantly or frequently takes a heavy toll on the body. There is a limit to the body's capacity to cope with that high alert response. Crossing that border exacts a toll. The cost accumulates and will invariably exact payment in emotional and physical ways.

Another piece of the puzzle involves the motivation for caring. This will be discussed in more detail later because it is a common element in most situations. Suffice it to say, one issue for Jordon was that his motivation to care came from both extrinsic and intrinsic motives. He was drawn to care for others by the great need he witnessed in them. Secondly, he was motivated by his love for the Lord and desire to serve him. These are extrinsic motives. On the other hand, he was driven to care by his intrinsic needs to be seen as a caring person. He developed a need to be affirmed for expressing compassion and to nurture the sensitivity that was inbred into him from an early age. Being driven exacts a high toll when it is a significant reason for entering the fast lane of caring for others. Sometimes the transition from extrinsic to intrinsic motives is very subtle.

Jordon accumulated a large debt resulting from excessive, prolonged, and very taxing engagement with hurting people. Physically and chemically, his body responded. The payment was exacted in emotional turmoil, confused thinking, and rumination. His mind circled the corral of his limited perspective. Soon, he was feeling very alone in his care.

Perhaps, one of the strongest indicators of emotional trouble is the painful experience (like Elijah) of feeling one is alone and isolated from community. The illusion of individuality cannot sustain this weight. Depression, sarcasm, blaming, judging others, and losing the awareness that God cares fosters despair and doubt. In this state, often one grasps at straws which may be opportunities to rise above the situation by entering too deeply and intensively into one very needy situation. The reciprocal response with Ruth was predictable given the dynamics they were each dealing with in their respective situations. That in no way relieves personal responsibility but it does help with understanding. And, understanding rather than judgment is what creates a future and remedial learning. This will be discussed further when we discuss the anatomy of failure.

Broken by Satan

No one's fall into sin can be discussed without considering the role of Satan. In the Scripture, Satan's role in human life is clearly acknowledged from Genesis to the Revelation of John. He injects his influence early in the story of Adam and Eve, and it is not until the victory of Christ in the Revelation that we see the end of his influence.

Importantly, man's responsibility for his actions is never erased by the actions of Satan. When we consider the attributes of Satan, man is a mismatch for his power. Yet man is accountable for his actions despite Satan's influence. For example, consider those situations where we are informed specifically of

Satan's role. Three of the most obvious are Adam and Eve, Job, Peter and Paul.

Consider the various descriptors that are used to describe him. I would list these in three groupings. In relation to people, he is called an accuser, adversary, tempter, and enemy of the souls of mankind.[126] In relation to power, he is the prince of demons, the prince of this world, the ruler of darkness, ruler of the kingdoms of the air, and the god of this age.[127] As to his function and behaviour, he is a murderer, the evil one, the serpent, and a liar.[128] This is quite a resume. All biblical writers, and no one more that Jesus, recognized the role of Satan in our world and in the lives of people. We need to note that it exists more than in the lives of individuals but also does so in communities, corporate entities, governments, and unseen powers. The presence of evil in the world cannot be denied nor adequately explained apart from the role of Satan. I will very briefly mention four aspects of the engagement of Satan in the world and the life of the believer.

The Performance of Satan

The Biblical picture evidences a pervasive impact. One need only look at the story of Adam and Eve. Very clearly in this story, the performance of Satan was to cast doubt concerning the complete goodness of God. He planted and nurtured the seeds of doubt. He fostered the sense of inadequacy by suggesting they could be more. He encouraged the incubation of a desire for greatness and increased knowledge, *"You will be like God, knowing good and evil."*[129] In the proper sense, to be like God would be desirable, but in another sense, it is diabolical. To have the knowledge of good and evil set up a conflict of great tension within man.

Paul references that conflict in his writing to the Romans. He declares that he knows good but does not have the power to do it.[130] And, that he also knows evil but does not have the power to resist doing what he really does wish to do. That knowledge cuts through the very heart of man. Our propensity to evil is evident in history and our own struggles. Therein lays our vulnerability. The dividing line between the influence of this internal conflict and the immediate role of Satan is very blurred. His subtlety is one of his chief characteristics. His attack is invariably at our weakest point, our most vulnerable time. C. S. Lewis captures his processes in *The Screwtape Letters,* and if you couple that with the *Abolition of Man,* you can better understand this interaction.[131]

In the case of David, the desires of the flesh were awakened in the context of the pursuit of leisure. Perhaps feeling more secure in his kingly role, maybe feeling exhausted, he did not go out to war. Retreating from his accustomed role as leader of his army, he did not know what to do with time on his hands and became a spectator to what prompted sinful desires. An equivalent in our day is seen in the number of pastors who become trapped in pornography. Often this occurs in times of leisure coupled with weariness in leadership. Satan taps into the desires of the flesh as a solution to many other issues and discouragements that lead to self-indulgence. The phrase Paul uses is *"delighted in wickedness"*[132]

The Persistence of Satan

In the story of Job, we see behind the scenes. Satan challenges God in suggesting that Job is only faithful because of the fruitfulness in his life, which he attributes to God. Strange to our ears, God gives permission to Satan to breach the "hedge" he claimed God had placed around Job. Satan received permission, although limited, to abuse Job. In a second confrontation, Satan receives permission to hurt Job physically but must spare his life. The perseverance of Satan and his use of the instrumentality of Job's friends to challenge Job adds much pressure. It is not only Satan but "friends" who function on Satan's behalf. They attacked Job with accusation, legalism, challenges of pride, and the labelling of being self-righteous.[133] One need not think long to remember that others, even friends, have related to us in ways that have prompted or facilitated yielding to sin. Satan's persistence continued over an extended time.

The patient persistence of Satan wears down resistance. It is the constant grinding on the soul that eventually makes it raw. The wear and tear of chronic pain, repetitive tragedy, recurring problems, and the unhelpful questioning, accusation or attack of friends breaks many fruitful boughs. Some have said of Job's friends, "With friends like that, who needs enemies!"

David also lamented such loss when he stated, "*My friends and companions stand aloof from my plague, and my nearest kin stand far off.*"[134] In David's situation, he was weak in body and seeking to avoid death at the hands of his enemies when he found that friends and family had also deserted him. Many things contribute to the wearing down of resistance and Satan knows all the tricks.

The Processes of Satan

Jesus indicates one of the chief processes of Satan is to sow tares among the wheat.[135] We are told that "*Satan rose up against Israel and incited David to take a census of Israel*" which greatly offended God.[136] Paul expresses his concern "*that Satan might not outwit us. For we are not unaware of his schemes.*"[137] He also refers to the "serpent's cunning" which leads minds astray.[138] In doing so, he can render Paul's efforts to be useless.[139] We are only told in Scripture of Peter's sifting and the painful experience this was for him. Jesus said, "*Simon, Simon, Satan has asked to sift you all as wheat.*"[140] I wonder about the story of the others.

Some of the processes of Satan are evidenced in the temptation of Jesus.[141] Satan encounters Jesus after forty days of fasting when he is physically weak, hungry, physiologically stressed, and alone in a harsh setting. There are many kinds of hunger such as social isolation, loneliness, feeling unloved, uncared for, or rejected. Emotional and social hunger are powerful in their ability to weaken our resistance to temptation. There are many needs for which we hunger. At that time, Satan tried to enter the life of Jesus through the avenue of need.

That being unsuccessful, he invited Jesus to expose himself to the risk of jumping off the temple, thus, challenging God's clear promise of care and protection. Many times, fruitful saints, whether in response to challenge or to evidence and illusion of great faith, test God. They may expose themselves to physical harm through overextension and high-risk behaviour or place themselves in a position where God would have to move unbelievers to fulfill their wishes. Putting out a "fleece" may have worked for Gideon but may be a questionable practice for those indwelled by the Holy Spirit.[142] The temptation to challenge God's faithfulness may be a tool of Satan.

Satan's third temptation focused on power, acclaim, acknowledgement, fame, control, and material success. The pride of position which may, in fact, be a compensation for insecurity, is an instrument in Satan's repertoire. These temptations are not easy to identify in ourselves and our capacity for rationalization is overwhelmingly subjective and subtle. The costs for responding to Satan's overtures are very high and destructive of God's purposes. One of the key words in Satan's vocabulary is that little word "if" which is the introduction to bargaining. It occurs several times in Satan's proposal. The rewards offered by Satan seem so appealing and sometimes so innocent. Frequently, there is a thread of truth hidden in the bargain offered.

The activity of Satan towards God's people is brutal. Paul speaks of that as being given *"a thorn in my flesh, a messenger of Satan, to torment me."*[143] This word is used in the treatment of Jesus as the soldiers beat him with their fists. Paul uses it to describe being "brutally treated" and Peter uses it in his description of being beaten.[144] Paul describes this as a "messenger of Satan." There is no gentleness in the treatment Satan dishes out to those who seek to serve God. We do not know specifically what the "thorn in my flesh" was for Paul but we have a clear sense of the pressure it brought upon him.

The Protection from Satan

It is clear from Scripture that Satan will ultimately be defeated. Paul assured the church at Rome that *"the God of peace will soon crush Satan under your feet.*"[145] The ultimate destruction of Satan and his emissaries is clearly presented both in terms of his present power and the eschatological fulfillment that John speaks of in his Revelation.[146] In the lives of both Job and Peter, Satan is limited in his capacity. In Job, God essentially says, "This far and no farther." Jesus assured Peter, *"I have prayed for you."*[147] The ongoing ministry of Jesus is explained by John when he says, *"We have an advocate with Father -Jesus Christ, the Righteous One."*[148] I think it is appropriate to assume that this intervention is not only when we sin but constantly.

James provides a clear understanding of our role in his epistles. *"Submit yourselves, then, to God. Resist the devil, and he will free from you. Come near to God and he will come near to you."*[149] We have a responsibility to seek purity, repentance, humility, and to avoid harmful relationships. This includes guarding the tongue, avoiding boasting, and seeking the ministry of the Spirit in patience and prayer. We are to live in communities where confession and mutual support enable us to be faithful. Seeking wisdom and avoiding quarrels and dissension in our communities of faith, will contribute to the control of our desires. In such a context, God will lift us up. Although we will experience temptations common to man, we can look to God for a way out.

Paul provides us with a reason for his thorn in the flesh. He sought the Lord three times for its removal. The Lord answered, *"My grace is sufficient for you, for my power is made perfect in weakness."*[150] The ultimate protection from Satan's buffeting is in the grace of God. The claiming of God's grace converts weaknesses into strengths. This is the testimony of the heroes of the faith *"whose weakness was turned into strength."*[151] We can also be assured that our Saviour is understanding, having been tempted, and has overcame in victory completely at the cross.[152]

Who can understand or withstand the wiles of Satan? In the seven stories related earlier, it was evident that many factors contributed to the brokenness that came into the lives of fruitful boughs who were serving God. One can readily see that the presenting issue that led to the movement out of ministry was only the tip of the iceberg. That is usually what is judged and dealt with in the dismissal or moving on of a servant of God. The Christian community may feel a real sense of righteous indignation, even a celebration of seeing a sinner getting what he deserves.

However, without exploring the contributing factors that led up to the final break, it is impossible to understand the situation. To focus on the precipitating cause may mean that we miss the contributing causes. Contributing causes may take us in many directions. Without understanding these, we encounter many other problems. Frequently, injustice is experienced, the real issues are not faced, repentance is not full or complete, and the potential for learning is lost. The contribution of family or community may not be recognized. There is no justice in overlooking the overt sin, but neither is there justice in overlooking the contributing causes.

There are many contributors to sin. Many come from within and many from outside the person. For the purpose of illustration, I have looked at stress, success, sensitivity and Satan in the role they may play in a pastor's failure. There may be many other contributors we will examine as we move forward.

Summary:

1. Stress, success, sensitivity and Satan are key players in these pastors' failures.
2. Behind these overt outcomes family dynamics, church leadership and influences from family of origin all played a role.
3. This raises questions of responsibility which we must address.

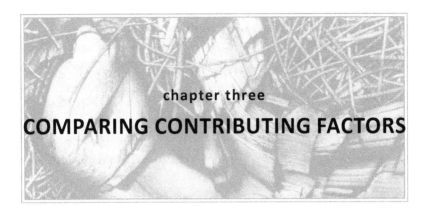

chapter three
COMPARING CONTRIBUTING FACTORS

IT WILL BE HELPFUL TO COMPARE SEVEN STORIES IN TERMS OF THEIR contributing factors. Each experience is different. However, there are definable patterns that are relatively consistent. The progress toward failure has considerable predictability. This is true at the emotional and physical level. We tend to be sufficiently different in personality, relational patterns and family functioning that there appears more variety as to the development of difficulty in these areas. This is also the case with the spiritual journey. The strength of one's spiritual discipline patterns may sustain one, or at least minimize awareness of developing difficulties. If one tends to "spiritualize" one's experience or define it in terms of "warfare" the interpretation changes the dynamic of sensitivity to the physical or emotional responses of the body. Grasping an understanding of the contributing influences is essential to preventing and intervening along the journey.

Biblical Men Comparison
In concluding the stories of the four Biblical characters, I provided a summary which identified some of the factors that many have contributed to their failure at the time of their fruitfulness. Let me list some of these in a chart form. It will facilitate our comparison of their experiences and the experiences of the stories I have told of fictional pastors.

Comparison of Biblical Persons	
Abraham	
• cultural dislocation • from plenty to famine • provision for family • unknown future • childlessness • infertility	• family friction in Lot and Sarah tension • wars all around • fear of Pharaoh • debate with God re Sodom • leadership demands
David	
• family tension • sibling rivalry • failure to lead in not going to war • leisure • companionship loss with soldiers	• loss of community • temperament • weariness of leadership • visual stimulation • loss of value perspective
Elijah	
• exhaustion from ministry, running • from success to fear • no rest or food • self-imposed isolation • loneliness	• loss of community and companions • discomfort of desert • no protection from elements • loss of faith in adversity
Peter	
• repeated reprimand • rejected leadership • exhaustion in the garden • disillusionment at the arrest • confused when no resistance accepted	• abandoned by his companions • sorrow seeing Christ abused • social pressure around the fire • fear for life • sifting of Satan

Figure 1.

The lists are partly conjecture on my part. However, if you imaginatively enter their experience and place yourself there you may sense the presence of these. One can readily see, from these suggestions, the similarity and differences in the experience of each of these biblical individuals. Understand, however, it is more difficult for us to project how their personality or their experience may have contributed. These could only be assessed with deep personal engagement, and they all lived centuries before us.

It is safe to assume that their personalities and experiences played a significant role. All our activity is shaped by personality and the behaviour patterns developed as we mature in our families. Our social environment is the habitation in which personality and behaviour are formed. Both our genetic predispositions and nurture have great impact in shaping our values, attitudes, desires, and the behaviour that is expressed.

It is important to keep in mind that we are not intending in any way to side-step the issue of personal responsibility for the behaviour of these four leaders. God addressed each of them in a different manner and a different focus. He did not remove either personal responsibility or consequences. At the same time, he did not abandon them.

He confronted Abraham, not directly, but in one situation through Pharaoh and in another from Abimelech. Other times, he dealt with Abraham directly. God sent Nathan to deal with David. Interestingly, Nathan approached David with a story. The function of the story was to arouse David to an awareness of the values that where of immense importance to him. It worked! David declared his values which might be expressed as fairness, justice, protection of the unprotected and his righteous indignation. Only after the clarification of those values did Nathan utter the words, he is so famous for, "Thou art the man!" The most effective confrontation only occurs after values that have been breached are clarified and declared.

The normal response when values have not been clarified is reaction, retreat, or rejection of responsibility. When the focus of confrontation is on the hurt or harm to the victim, the response is usually justification. When values are first clarified, the persons being confronted must deal with their breach of their own values. If they have made a commitment to God's values, then the issue is between them and God. Of course, both may be the case. Simply put, judgment leads to reaction. Clarification of values, through understanding, more frequently leads to acknowledgement of guilt.

God dealt with Elijah directly by addressing his physical needs, his exhaustion, and his mis-information about the community of prophets that he should have known about. Frequently, when great physical needs are present, they need to be addressed before the deeper needs are, such as emotional, attitudinal, or spiritual. An African proverb says, "A hungry belly has no ears!" God had to rescue Elijah from his physical need before dealing with deeper issues.

God responds to people according to a hierarchy of needs. This is consistent with the modern understanding of our hierarchy of values. Remember how God addressed Moses in dealing with his sense of inadequacy for God's calling by focusing on God's involvement in his life and ministry? Or, we could look at his confrontation of Jonah about his elitism, racial prejudice, and blatant, willful disobedience.[153]

In his encounter with Peter after his resurrection, Jesus focused on two things —Peter's love for him and his need to obey without being concerned with John's responsibility.[154] Jesus had earlier assured Peter of his prayer for him in the face of Satan's sifting. We do not know to what extent he discussed with Peter his fall in denying he knew Jesus, but that is less important. Each situation is dealt with in terms of the needs of each person. God personalizes his response. He responds in confrontation or discipline in terms of the need and experience of each person.

Modern Boughs Broken Comparison

We will explore the experience of Jim, Mel, and Jordon in a different manner. You will understand that I created these stories to maintain confidentiality but also to illustrate the complexity and the multiplicity of contributors to the brokenness experience by pastors and others in ministry Since these stories are a compilation of the experience of scores of pastors with whom I have journeyed in depth, I can provide a clearer picture with more detail. With many individuals, we were able to use appropriate psychological and vocational testing to explore personality, family relationships, developmental experiences, etc. Before elaborating, let me provide a broad perspective. This is a very brief synopsis of some of the differences in the experience of Jim, Mel, and Jordon. These will be explored in more detail in our examination of the different journeys that constitute the journey toward failure in Chapter 4. We will, at that time, look more closely at some of the contributing factors to bring some order to the chaos that became part of the lives of these men in ministry.

I have listed the contributing factors, in some measure, in the sequence in which they became involved in each life. In any one of these situations, the pastor may have succumbed to the experience of stress experienced in their bodies. However, frequently the dedication and commitment to ministry will often result in an accumulation of stress until moral failure occurs. Action is not taken until desperation sets in. There are usually many evidences of physical distress, aloneness, feelings of failure, spousal or family issues and withdrawal into secret grieving before moral failure occurs.

Fruitful boughs break for many reasons. We must look at more than the breakage to determine preventive measures that might forestall such undesirable outcomes. These will be explored by seeking processes of understanding, by examining the different elements in the journey toward failure, and in specific contributing factors to failure.

Comparison of Modern Fruitful Boughs Broken

Broken by Stress: Jim

• hidden conflict in board • competition among elders • financial pressure re family • feeling of not providing • measuring faith by works • overwhelming demands • tensions with legalists • lack of skills to uncover hidden tensions • feelings of inadequacy • focus on needs of others rather than self or family • outcomes of chronic stress	• self-doubt, fatigue, emotional exhaustion • frustration expressed in anger, sarcasm • breaching values increased his sense of worth • self-nurturing, feeling sorry for self • isolation, aloneness • secrecy • fear of being found out • panic; quick decision • shared secrecy with wife • escape

Broken by Success: Mel

• a model of success to follow • constant affirmation created a need for approval • giftedness led to opportunity • absence of mentoring or supervision • quick & rapid growth, little time for reflection • loss of contact with congregation • pressure of board demands • team conflicts re resources, desire for his attention • demand for access from associates	• family discord, tension, no time with family • pressure from consultant • feeling inadequate, must be more to ministry • demands of administration • internalization of anger, frustration • inability to meet expectations: home, church • medical issues • loneliness, despair, depression • withdrawal of wife • unacknowledged depression • finally, a listening ear

Comparison of Modern Fruitful Boughs Broken	
Broken by Sensitivity: Jordon	
• a model of compassion	• stomach problems
• exposure to a massive culture of need	• rumination
• crossing cultures from farm to urban inner city	• more demands
• constant encounter of irresolvable problems	• consumed by compassion
• wallowing in unmet personal needs	• rejection by church leaders
• feeling no one cared for him	• feeling misunderstood, unappreciated
• loss of God consciousness	• isolation from community
• fear of "going crazy"	• feeling abandoned by church
• false guilt	• financial pressure
• confused thinking	• white lies to cover
• sleep disturbances	• self-deception
	• secrecy
	• transference and counter-transference

Figure 2

Paul accused some people in Corinth of "judging by appearances"[155] To respond to one bad decision, as if it were the whole, is irresponsible. Misbehavior is only the tip of the iceberg. The mass of the problem lies below the surface activity. When things break down, we may become aware of what we have failed to attend to what lead up to the breakage. A car that is not maintained will soon manifest inadequate care. We know this is true with physical health as well as emotional health.

Passing immediate moral judgment usually bypasses understanding and involves the application of laws or regulations in a black or white fashion. From the beginning of this book, we indicated our attempt was to understand. To focus on the incident of moral failure without understanding the many contributing factors is much too simple.

In order to achieve understanding, discernment is required. We must lay side by side the many and varied inputs to a person's life. Decisions are best made when at least a reasonable level of understanding of what has preceded the incident of failure has been achieved. I cannot stress too much the importance of seeking understanding before decisions are made. To respond to a situation in terms of the specific incident is like buying a car simply because the shell looks nice. A superficial view is at best pre-judgment and worst destructive and inhibitive of learning. Every piece of new understanding has the potential for learning and the power to initiate new behaviour.

There are several perspectives from which one must explore the lives of individuals. It is very important to understand the *spiritual dimension* which would involve one's spiritual life, one's moral commitments, the values that provide direction, the strength of one's commitment to follow what one believes God's will to be, and the natural and spiritual gifts of the person. One must also consider the *physical functioning* of the individual from the perspective of health, biological variables, the influence of disease, if present, and any genetic predispositions. The *psychological assessment* would include the presence of stress, emotional capacity to cope, the attitudes that are imbedded in the personality, the strength or weakness of the will, and many other aspects that will have become part of the person's functioning. The *social functioning* of the person will dramatically influence behaviour. For example, whether the person is an introvert or extrovert, communicative withholds in conversation, is affectively expressive or not, and many other considerations. Understanding behaviour should involve a multi-dimensional understanding of the individual.

The priority is to understand, exploring all the contributors which led to the failure. They will vary from person to person. For example, when a pastor is referred to me, I will often request contact with church leadership as a possibility in the future. Fairly frequently, it will be evident that physical illness or depression is present. It may be important to address these first by referral to a medical specialist. Medical issues or psychiatric concerns, if not addressed first, will interfere with our journey to explore the spiritual, relational, social, or personality considerations that have expressed themselves in the behaviour that became the focus of attention. These must be understood before the church dynamics in which the behaviour occurred can be understood. There will be an interactive correlation between all these variables.

Indicators of Stress and Burnout

Many times, we were able to explore in depth various relationships within the churches. We may meet with entire church groups, elder boards, deacons, and others intimately involved in the lives of pastors. Spouses and children were often a part of the counselling process.

Over the years, I have developed simple instruments that evidence recurring elements in many situations. Two of those follow in chart form to provide an overview. The one identifies "Personal Indicators of Stress" (see figure 3) and the other "Contributors to Pastoral Burnout." (see figure 4)

Stress in one of the areas indicated is often manageable for a time. However, these are interactive and dynamically affect each other. A person's behaviour changes in response to health issues and can cause relationship tension. Spiritual malaise impacts all areas. It is helpful to have both spouses complete one of these forms on each other and compare the results. Placing a time-line of the awareness showing when a spouse noticed an occurrence in one or more of these areas can be very helpful. The exploration of these variables is immensely important.

Personal Indicators of Stress
(Glenn C. Taylor, 1991)

Health Indicators

- ☐ fatigue & chronic exhaustion
- ☐ frequent & prolonged colds
- ☐ headaches (tension or migraine)
- ☐ sleep disturbances
  - -insomnia
  - -nightmares
  - -excessive sleeping
- ☐ gastro-intestinal disorders
- ☐ ulcers
- ☐ hypertension
- ☐ heart disease
- ☐ vague viral-like symptoms
- ☐ muscle or skeletal pain
- ☐ sudden loss or gain of weight
- ☐ flare-up of pre-existing problems
- ☐ increased premenstrual tension
- ☐ injuries from high risk behaviour
- ☐ excessive sweating or urination

Behaviour Indicators

- ☐ nervous behaviour
- ☐ extreme mood or behavioral changes
- ☐ increase use of addictive substances
- ☐ high risk-taking behaviour
- ☐ hyperactivity
- ☐ change in sexual behaviour or dysfunction
- ☐ withdrawal from activity
- ☐ over or under eating

Emotional Adjustment Indicators

- ☐ emotional distancing
- ☐ paranoia
- ☐ depression, sadness, discouragement
- ☐ smolderivng resentment
- ☐ decreased emotional control
- ☐ martyrdom
- ☐ fear of 'going crazy'
- ☐ increased amount of daydreaming/fantasy
- ☐ constant sense of being 'trapped'
- ☐ undefined fears
- ☐ inability to concentrate
- ☐ regression

Relationship Indicators	
☐ isolation from, or over-bonding with others	☐ increased interpersonal conflict
☐ general critical attitude	☐ reversals of usual behaviour
☐ irritability, impatience, hatred	☐ mistrust of friends or family
☐ rebellion against authority	☐ inability to make decision
☐ immoral behaviour	☐ forgetfulness of appointments, deadlines, etc.
☐ increased marital or family conflict	
Attitude Indicators	
☐ self-condemnation	☐ attitudes of self-righteousness
☐ sense of total inadequacy	☐ hypercritical of organizations or peers
☐ frequent spells of brooding	☐ demonstrations of despair
☐ boredom	☐ expressions of false guilt
☐ sick sense of humor	☐ overwhelming sense of loss or grief
☐ 'tragic sense of life' attitude	
Spiritual Value Indicators	
☐ loss of faith	☐ spiritualizing of problems that may be physical, emotional or medical
☐ spiritual crisis	
☐ sudden & extreme changes in values or beliefs	☐ withdrawal from, or critical of one's faith community
☐ loss of hope or loss of anticipation	☐ movement to legalism, rigidity, critical attitude
☐ blaming God	☐ movement into 'cults' or submissiveness or denial of responsibility for self

Figure 3.

You will see that Figure 4 is a compilation of things we have found that contribute to burnout. Each of these requires exploration and assessment. There is a great deal of similarity between the experience of pastors who fail and those who experience post-traumatic stress disorder while servicing in theaters of war. When we consider Paul's exhortation about putting on the whole armor of God in dealing with the wiles of the devil, this may be expected.

Contributors to Pastoral Burnout	
I. Baggage from the Past	
1. Residual Issues from Family of Origin • self-image; sibling rivalry; self-image	2. Relational Patterns • sociability; communication; problem-solving; emotional intelligence; social intelligence 3. Cultural Influences • frugality; ethnicity
II. Ministry Expectations	
1. Impact of Educational Experience – scholarship vs pastoral model	2. Evangelism vs Discipleship - birthing vs growing people 3. Expectation of honor, leadership
III. Conflict Encounters	
1. Problem-solving issues 2. Stress Responses to Tension	3. Lack of Clarity in Identify priority issues
IV. Leadership Issues	
1. Leadership Expectations – authority, power, influence, leadership from behind	2. Changing Leadership in Growing congregations 3. Delegation Issues

V. Challenges to Success	
1. Defining success – success vs obedience, numbers game 2. Disciples Distraction – competition vs complementarity	3. Expectations of Others – denomination
VI. Transitions in Ministry	
1. Knowing God's will – God's calling vs church call 2. Personal vs family concerns	3. Evaluating One's ministry 4. Stages of Life and Ministry
VII. Health Issues	
1. Assessing health issues – stress or aging	2. Maintaining wellness – self-care, family care

Figure 4.

To achieve understanding, one must explore all contributing factors. This very broad stroke overview may help as we consider the experiences of Jim, Mel, and Jordon. We will look at their experience through this grid.

It may be most helpful to see the similarities and differences in the experience of these three men. Their origins were different as where their personalities. Families of origin, expectations, interpersonal skills, gifts of the Spirit, and their understanding and attitudes to ministry were distinct. There are some similarities in the process and outcomes, but these were modified by other variables. In each case, moral failure resulted but the responses to moral failure varied. We want to see if we can achieve understanding to maximize learning. As indicated earlier, there is no attempt to dispute the reality of sin, but we are trying to understand the "why" of this outcome.

Seeking Understanding of Failure and Sin

We have shared four stories from the Bible of fruitful boughs broken. We have also shared the stories of three pastors who were also fruitful boughs broken. The metaphor has been that of a tree bearing fruit. The branches became so overloaded that the boughs broke. The weight of the fruit contributed to the breaking. However, there were many other contributing factors. If we continued this analogy, we would examine many other considerations. These would include the nature of the tree, its ancestry, the failure in care such as pruning, limiting the fruit to increase quality, and all the other factors that go into creating a healthy orchard.[156]

Termination is most often the outcome chosen as appropriate. It may be decided by the board, the church or the pastor. Moral failure must be addressed.

As I have said earlier, in the Biblical stories, such as David's, the consequences of his failure continued for the remainder of his life. He did not lose his relationship with God but suffered much pain in his family. Most frequently when pastors experience failure their ministry is terminated. I am not arguing that should not be the case. Most often, failure in ministry leads to a necessary ending[157] of that ministry. The tragedy is that these endings in failure lead to dire consequences, but rarely do they lead to the learning that they have the potential to offer. Nor do they lead to the redemptive outcomes illustrated in the biblical stories. Rarely are they explored in terms of prevention, earlier intervention, or healing for those tragically affected by them. Churches are left in disarray, pain, grief, loss of trust, disillusionment, and, sometimes a tragic sense of self-righteousness for having addressed immorality. Pastors and their families are plunged into crises. Children are confused emotionally and spiritually bruised by their ignorance of what has happened and by their experience of seeing (from their limited perspective) their parents broken. The experience of the children is not often considered. They suffer transitions, dislocation in homes, schools, friendships, etc. More frequently than not, pastors remain broken, living in despair, inadequately equipped for an alternative vocation and overpowered by shame and guilt.

These outcomes for churches, pastors, and their families may be mitigated. There are viable alternatives. Perhaps, the most important place to start is to understand that, whatever the consequences of the failure, it should be viewed as the outcome of a journey, not an isolated incident. Failure is never an isolated incident. Every failure has antecedents. There are precursors to failure. It is not possible to comprehend failure without considering what leads up to that drastic outcome. Therefore, it is crucial for us to explore the journey toward failure. Before seeking to understand the journey, let us look at the understanding of failure and sin.

Perspectives on Failure

Before exploring the antecedents to failure, it will be helpful to identify the perspectives that characterize our interpretation of failure. Failure is multi-faceted and is open to many interpretations depending on the perspective from which it is viewed. We have all chuckled when someone has quipped, "The devil made me do it!" Obviously, from a theological perspective, there is much truth in that, as we indicated in the section headed, "Broken by Satan." There are many other perspectives, also. These are frequently found in secular literature in a discussion of the causes of burnout.[158] For our purposes, I will briefly summarize these.

Authoritarian-Moral Approach

This approach assumes what would theologically be described as the fallenness of man. Man is a moral creature, capable of choice, who will frequently choose evil or unhelpful responses rather than seeking the good or the holy. Thus, failure is seen in terms of character flaws, moral failure, spiritual weakness, or the unwillingness to choose what is right or what is desired by those in authority.

1. *Cognitive Approach*: This approach will focus on understanding failure as unrealistic thinking, irrational thinking, ideas, beliefs, or expectations about oneself or others. This may be attributed to faulty socialization, lack of knowledge, or a deficiency in ability.
2. *Clinical Approach*: The focus here will be on emotional and relational problems arising from

personality variables. These lead to ineffective or inefficient functioning either personally or socially which, in turn, lead to failure and frustration in the community. The emergence of the problem is from within the individual.

3. *Training Approach*: In this approach, the focus is on failure arising from inadequate skills, training, or the discrepancy between the individual's gifts or abilities and those demanded by the challenge of the task at hand. Performance is measured against expectations and the person is found incapable of fulfilling those expectations.

4. *Environmental Approach*: In this case, the failure is defined in terms of the work environment. The organizational structure, lines of communication, authority patterns, or ineffective policies are considered the cause of the failure. There are organizational structures that are more prone to the production of failure.

5. *Systems Approach*: Here the failure is seen as an outcome of a breakdown in the relationship between the individual and the organization. The ecology of the organization is studied as a complex expression of this relationship which may involve personal issues, role considerations, process problems, exterior influences on the organization or political, economic, or social influences.

There is much help in seeking to understand the failure from these different perspectives. However, one must also understand that a biblical perspective must see the brokenness of our experience from the perspective of sin.

A Theological Perspective of Failure and Sin
The Scriptures employ different words to distinguish between failure and sin. Failure might be defined as leaving something out

(that should be there), or indicating something insufficient for the intended purpose, or of something not having adequate force to accomplish what was intended. It is essentially a deficiency, but it might not be a moral deficiency. Sin is defined very differently. In presenting an understanding of sin, there are three very important considerations. These can only be briefly defined here as they bear on our discussion.

The Role of Satan
In the section of Chapter 2 entitled, "Broken by Satan," I outlined the biblical aspect of Satan's activity. This is best illustrated in the stories of Adam and Eve, Job's trials, and the temptation of Jesus. Zechariah presents a vivid picture: "*Then he showed me Joshua the high priest standing before the angel of the Lord, and Satan standing at his right hand to accuse him.*"[159] In Mathew thirteen, Jesus presents parables outlining the role of Satan in the world. Paul clearly outlines the protection that is needed to deal with Satan's abuse.[160] John, the Apostle declares, "*The one who does what is sinful is of the devil, because the devil has been sinning from the beginning.*"[161] When considering the experience of pastors who are tempted and fail, we must consider the role of Satan. You may wish to re-read this section in light of this discussion.

The Personal Nature of Sin
Beginning with Adam and Eve, mankind is held responsible for his/her personal sin. The sinful nature of man came because of the fall of mankind, which involved many dimensions of sin including disobedience, fear and hiding from God, the prideful reach for likeness to God, the interpersonal conflict and accusation of each other, and the pursuit of individual interests at the expense of others. The sinful nature of man is passed from generation to generation, inclusive of all. "All are under sin."[162]

Sin is often described as missing the mark by which we mean failing to live up to the laws of God. This inner inclination leads to covetous desire, conflict, death and, apart from grace, separation from God. It is the nature of man to sin in behavioural, mental, and relational ways. The self, apart from Christ, is described as the "old self...slaves to sin."[163] The Apostle John declared, "Everyone who sins breaks the law." (1 John 3:4) Sin is a breach of God's law and every individual is found personally guilty. Sin arises from within and expresses itself pervasively through man's thoughts, desires, and behaviour. Despite the role of Satan, man is considered responsible for his sin.

The Inner Nature of Sin

It is of great importance to differentiate the behaviour of sin and the inner nature of sin. When people respond to the behaviours of sin and assume they have dealt with sin, they may be misled. The nature of sin is imbedded in our being. The change or eradication of sinful actions does not necessarily mean a change of heart or a new birth in the Spirit. One may change behaviour for many reasons rather than from a change of heart. Consider the example of Jesus. He, in his temptation by Satan, shifted Satan's focus from food, fame and fatherly protection to the heart issue that was involved in each case. In the case of the Rich Young Man who had no consciousness of sinful behaviour, assuming he had kept all the commandments, Jesus led him to address the issues of his heart which was more focused on his retention of wealth than on spiritual issues. When the Pharisees brought the woman taken in adultery to Jesus, they appeared to be preoccupied with her sin but not their own. Presumably, she was aware of her sin having been caught in it. The response of Jesus was to focus not on her sin but on theirs while urging her to sin no more. On other occasions he challenged the Pharisees: "Why are you thinking these things in your hearts?" (Luke 5:27) He seemed not to have a problem associating with those who practised sinful behaviour whether they where aware of their behaviour or not. However, in dealing Simon (Luke 7), the contrast of his dealing with the woman anointing his feet with perfume, whom everyone knew to be a sinner, and Simon who appeared to have no awareness of need for forgiveness is stark. He saw the heart of widow who gave her few pennies and the contrast with those who gave with showmanship. Jesus habitually looked behind sinful behaviour to examine the contributors to sin. Behaviour may be a distraction from dealing with the real issue.

The Corporate Nature of Sin

Sin is so pervasive that if contaminates all cultures created by mankind. Indeed, one of Satan's primary functions is his guidance and direction of the kingdoms of the world. The cultural and communal dimension of sin places great pressure on all of us. Satan is operative in the cultural, political, and human interactions of the world. Corporate sin is best understood by studying the relationship of God with the community of Israel. God entered a communal relationship of obedience with Adam and Eve, and entered a communal, redemptive relationship with Israel. Two relationships define the real nature and identity of man. One is his relationship and responsibility toward God, and the second is his relationship and responsibility toward his fellowmen. Jesus summarized this as the First and Second Commandments: Love of God and love of neighbour.

We must acknowledge that the current understanding of the person as an "autonomous individual" or "unencumbered self" who is free to create himself as he chooses, even to the extent of choosing his identity, is a modern creation.[164] This imagined independence bears no correlation to the reality of a biological or relational experience. The Scripture sees man as a member of a covenant community where he exists in relation to God and in interdependence with his fellowman. He does not stand apart from his relationship with God or others. In the community of Israel, the interdependence was so clear that sometimes the community was held responsible for the sin of the individual and sometimes the individual was held responsible for the actions of the community. Either the individual or the community could lead the other to sin. This interdependence was pictured in the New Testament in the image of the body as descriptive of our relationship, responsibility, and dependence upon each other.[165] Our care for each other is an essential requirement of our faith communities.

It is in the light of this interdependence that we understand the teaching of Jesus wherein he pronounced woe on anyone who caused another to sin.[166] This corporate responsibility is evidenced in Paul's argument about not causing one's fellow-believer to stumble. The image here is of placing a block before a blind man or setting a trap or obstacle before another.[167] Sometimes there are those who place obstacles in the paths of others.[168] In his parable of the weeds sown among good seeds, Jesus reveals "weeds" to mean *"the weeds are the people of the evil one."*[169] We will elaborate on the communal dimension of sin in our discussion of the church community's role in pastoral failure later in this chapter.

It becomes very evident that sin arises from many sources. Satan, man's sinful nature, the influence of others, and the culture of the community of which we are a part can all lead to sin. Man does not stand alone in choosing his being, identity, or behaviour. People in a community of faith are responsible for each other and mutually interdependent. True, the individual is not without blame and is accountable. However, the community does not stand apart from the sin of its members and may be a strong contributor to the sin of its members. The culture of all communities, even churches, is permeated with evil influences. Who can measure guilt? When a member sins, only God can determine the responsibility of the individual, the community, or Satan. I suspect it is for this reason that Paul states, *"I care very little if I am judged by you or any human court; indeed, I do not even judge myself. My conscience is clear, but that does not make me innocent."*[170] He goes on to say that only when the Lord comes will what is hidden be exposed and the motives of man's heart known.

The Church's Response to Sin
Obviously, in the meantime churches must deal with the matter of discipline and respond to the failure of pastors when these fruitful

boughs in ministry are broken. Paul's instruction to the church in Corinth indicates that the appropriate response to moral sin in the church is exclusion.[171] We should hasten to add that there was also an injunction to restore the person.[172] To fail in restoration would lead to a soul-damaging rejection of the brother and a failure to thwart Satan's schemes. We will come back to this crucial process.

In counselling with pastors who have experienced brokenness in ministry, I have found it helpful to begin by tentatively discussing the outcome that has brought termination or conflict. Virtually all pastors acknowledge that relationships have been broken. I do not prejudge the situation by labeling it as either a failure or sin. Only after careful examination of all the factors, identified and understood, is it possible to offer any conclusion. It is the work of the Holy Spirit to employ conviction. Once we have prayerfully, with humility in the safety of a confidential relationship, become aware of the degree to which failure or sin may be involved, then we can define the issue. Seeking the guidance of the Spirit of God, a pastor will arrive at his conviction of sin and his responsibility in all the outcomes of this rupture in relationship. It is only when that depth of understanding is achieved can true repentance be expressed. When that is achieved, it becomes important to move on to grasp the grace of God in forgiveness and restoration. Restoration begins with restoration of the pastor's relationship with God. But then, we must deal with reconciliation in relation to any spouse, children, church community, social community, and address any other needs for reconciliation. We do not discuss restoration to ministry in this process. The more important and foundational issues must be addressed first. It is of great importance that this process not be short-circuited.

A safe environment where one can plumb the depths of one's soul to find the humility and grace to understand one's personal role, as well as the role of others, is crucial. It is necessary to view the role or contribution of others, not as an escape from one's own responsibility, but rather to see it in a non-judgemental way. If, as sometimes happens, the elders' board or church community are open to exploring their role then the possibility for learning and growth exponentially increases. However, this opportunity is lost if the church leadership are not engaged in the process or if they refuse to participate in achieving understanding of the journey that led to this tragic outcome.

The Role of Churches in Pastoral Failure

Any reasonable and unbiased student of history will recognize the reality that Christianity has contributed immensely to the development of governing principles. These principles have, without a doubt, improved the opportunities for the common man. Also, most will readily recognize the role of Christians in leading in reform in many areas including education, penal and health reform, and the promotion of moral values in society. Much of the motivation for modern science was initiated and promoted by individuals deeply committed to Christianity. The church and its members have had great influence throughout the course of history. It has been salt and light in the world.

Throughout much of recent history, however, the principle of the separation of church and state has lessened the role of the church in society. Fear of the "social gospel" and liberal theology has discouraged many evangelicals from engaging in social justice or response to the plights of the poor.

If one looks at churches as Christian communities, it is appropriate to ask about the changes in expectations with respect to behaviour or moral intentions within those communities. Of course, with the very great differences existing today in church communities, it is not possible to generalize. Since my involvement has been with several denominations that would be considered broadly evangelical, I will limit my discussion to those. It is from that group of denominations that the pastors and others in ministry have come to me for counsel or consultation.

For many of those, there is a desire to replicate the motives, functions, and expectation that one would find to have characterized the churches of the New Testament. Many look to these churches as providing a model to pursue. Some only emphasize the doctrinal commitment. It is legitimate to ask whether churches function today, as did the New Testament churches. My focus is not on doctrinal similarity but rather the similarity or differences evidenced in the behaviour and relationships in churches.

The Church's Identity

Many times, in Scripture, the reference is to the Church as inclusive of all believers of all ages. The Church is divinely instituted, and Christ is the Head of the Church. It is referred to as the Church of God, the Bride of Christ, and the Family of God. Its members are known as the children of God.[173] The members of the Church are described either as branches who must be attached to the vine in order to be fruitful or as a flock under the care of the Good Shepherd. Members are also referred to as a temple to be indwelled by the Holy Spirit.

Interestingly, the terminology used is commonly referred to as the Church Universal as well as for local, individual churches. Each church bears the identity of the whole. This makes the relationship of each church with God very personal. Some insist on the autonomy of each individual church. The relationship of everyone in the congregation is also described in these very personal and intimate terms. There is a uniqueness in this which cannot be replicated in any corporate organization.

Personally, I see this as the foundation on which the expectation for unity resides. Unity is accomplished by the Holy Spirit which indwells the individual, in each church, and through the Church, which is composed of all the people of faith from all ages. When one focuses on the identity of the Church from this perspective it places the Church in a very crucial role. The Roman Catholic tradition presents the Church as God's representative and as having considerable authority. The authority of the Church is expressed very differently in one denomination as compared to another. This is evident in denominations that are structured to have denominational authority taking precedence over local church authority. Many seek a balance between the individual as he/she stands before God and the church community as it expresses and functions with authority. The tension becomes evident when one discusses the role of church discipline in the lives of its members or the responsibility of the church for the behaviour of its membership. The understanding we have of the relationship of a local church to the denomination impacts the expression of discipline of individual pastors.

Paul expresses the role of the church in its witness: *"God... created all things. His intent was that now, through the church, the manifold wisdom of God should be made known to the rulers and authorities in the heavenly realms, according to his eternal purposes which he accomplished in Christ Jesus our Lord."*[174] This is a high and holy calling. It becomes clear that *"the manifold wisdom of God"* will be made known by the quality of the relationships made possible by the resurrected Saviour and the enabling of his Spirit. This is a huge expectation and motivation by which a church's behaviour is to be determined.

The Church in its Relationships

A common analogy is to describe the "church" as a body or a building. These analogies are adequately explained to provide the intended meaning.[175] The members are described as brothers and sisters who have a crucial responsibility in caring for one another.[176] They are to see themselves as having all been adopted into one family; God's family. As such, they are to have equal care for all, showing no favouritism, no competition, and no divisions. They are heirs together of the grace of God. They are to bear one another's burdens, provide financial assistance when needed, both for each other and especially the poor. When there are weak members among them, they are to encourage, affirm, and build up one another.[177] Together, they are to rejoice and weep as appropriate. Forgiveness, love, gratitude, and praise are to be the major themes in their relationship and worship.[178] As they look to each other's needs and care for each other, they will fulfil

God's plan for a community of faith. Negative emotions, such as anger, rage, malice, filthy talk, and malice, are to be eliminated.[179] Prayer, teaching, effective witness, praise, and honesty are to express the culture of the community.

All the above are to be pursued through the ministry of the Holy Spirit and his enabling. Growth into the fullness and maturity of Christ will enable them to live lives worthy of the Lord. Changing one's thinking, one's priorities, and one's pursuit of Christ is to be the passion and motivation that drives the community, both individually and corporately. A commitment to Christ leads to self-control and to the disciplines that evidence priority of love for Christ and obedience to the heavenly Father.[180] The sanctifying work of the Spirit is founded upon knowing the truth of Scripture.

It is evident that the quality of relationship anticipated in each church and among churches was an exception of great magnitude amongst all the cultures that surrounded the Mediterranean Sea in that first century. Relationships directed toward the benefit of others resulted in believers standing out as being very different from their cultures. The care of the churches for each other was unique. A study of the contrast between the secular cultures in which the churches were embedded and what characterized the relationships in the Church is a worthy study. The power of the witness of the Church in the first century was amazing. *"Behold, how these Christians loved one another"* seemed a common response. The Mediterranean basin became infiltrated with churches during the first century. They were on a mission to fulfill the commission of Christ, the Head of the Church.

Today, however, we seem to seek to be more like the surrounding culture, as is evidenced in our church organizational structures and our "theatre like" worship centres.

The Church's Real Life

The ideals of church life were explicit and expounded by the leadership. However, the real life of the Church did not always measure up to the ideal. The Gospel was presented to legalistic Jews and pagans from all cultures. The problem arose in bringing people, both pagans and those self-righteously claiming to have favour with God, to maturity in Christ. The distance from paganism and religiosity to maturity in Christ was a long and arduous road to traverse. In many cases, people moved along the pathway to sanctification very slowly. Thus, in the churches could be found believers who lived lives worthy of Christ and some who, driven by other motives and immaturity, were a hindrance to the church. It is apparent that the resisters to growing in Christ had different motivations and desires. There were those influenced by pagan philosophy. The presence of those steeped and stuck in deep tradition became a major issue. The church was a cultural mixture. This was what the Apostles and pastors dealt with day to day.

Thus, we find the unvarnished picture of New Testament churches fraught with issues. There is no attempt to cover up or pretend it didn't exist. A real picture is presented in scripture.

In the church at Ephesus, for example, there was false doctrine and meaningless talk as people argued about endless genealogies. Names such as Hymanaeus and Alexander are given as examples. There were those who indulged in ungodly behaviour which spread like gangrene and there were those who loved this world.[181]

The church in Crete included rebellious people who were ruining whole households.[182] Corinth experienced divisions, arrogance, immorality, law suits among believers, quarrelling, outburst of anger, and debauchery.[183] They became stuck in the competitive distraction of the disciples, in which they developed preferences for various preachers, thus, creating divisions. The church members in Galatia are accused by Paul of devouring each other with provocation and envy.[184] If one turns to the churches addressed in John's Revelation you discover they are charged with different issues for which they need repentance.[185]

Obviously, the church members did not all live up to the ideal of the sanctification to which the Spirit of God was seeking to lead them. The human nature of early believers created issues and resistance to a teaching that sought the renewal of mind as well as a dramatic change in behaviour. It does not help us today to idealize the churches of the New Testament. Rather, we have much to learn from the pressures of those in ministry and how they coped with the reality of members continuing in sin.

Ministry in the Context of Imperfection

Paul, Peter, James, Jude, and all of those who ministered in the context of these churches faced what they were dealing with squarely and honestly. The impact on them was great. Perhaps, none have been so articulate as Paul on how deeply the problems within his churches affected him. The intensity of his commitment cannot be questioned. *"Besides everything else, I face daily the pressure of my concern for all the churches,"* he writes.[186] *"Night and day we pray most earnestly that we may see you again and supply what is lacking in your faith."*[187] He says, *"We were under great pressure, far beyond our ability to endure."*[188] When he was in Macedonia he acknowledges, *"We had no rest, but we were harassed at every turn – conflicts on the outside, fears within. But God, who comforts the downcast, comforted us by the coming of Titus."*[189]

Paul urged the churches to address the issues in their midst, warning them and motivating them to walk in a manner worthy of Christ. The pressure he experienced was great. It appears that his concern for the morality and growth of the Church created more problems for him than did the persecution and imprisonments he experienced.

How is it possible to maintain one's equilibrium in the face of such pressures? It is helpful to note that Paul's depression was lifted by a fellow pastor, Titus.[190] The weariness, emotional exhaustion, and physical demands of ministering to believers coming from all stations in life pressed upon the teachers and Apostles. Their intimate involvement in people's lives and their conflicts was constant. Paul, eventually, gathered around him a task force which he sent from place to place to deal with immorality, doctrinal dissension, and intermittent conflict. It is difficult to imagine that the New Testament churches knew anything about the concept of autonomy of individual churches that often inhibits mutual care of churches for each other. Competing for members seems more characteristic of churches today. This does not seem to be present in first century churches. They expressly care for each other.[191] The church was a mixed group. Some people were motivated by personal issues or doctrinal perspectives existing outside the teachings of the Apostles. Relational tensions required addressing. The membership of the churches represented the whole spectrum of human cultures.

It is important to notice that issues arose, not simply from immature members but also from leaders. Elders were appointed in each church. There were high qualifications for their role. Other leaders, whether self-appointed or chosen, often appeared to have contributed to the tensions and pressures the Apostles dealt with in their ministry. My purpose is simply to recognize that what pastors experience today may not differ much from what was experienced in the New Testament churches. People do not change quickly from paganism or religiosity to become followers of Christ. Churches contribute significantly to the experience of pastors in numerous ways. It has become clear to me that these contributors play a significant role in the breaking of fruitful boughs. Pastors are not exempt from these pressures. We do well to look at their impact on those called of God to ministry.

Leadership Issues Provide Tensions

Tension among leaders was an element in New Testament times. Personality appears to play a significant role in shaping leadership expectations. This is a large topic. Indeed, too large to be addressed at this point. We must come back to this vital issue in chapter five.

However, let me indicate that I do not see the concept of authority, which gets large press today in discussion of leadership, playing that role in the early churches. Paul does not lead from a position of authority. He uses the imagery of a gentle mother and an encouraging father to describe his leadership.[192] He presents some of his recommendations with significant tentativeness.[193] He models a cooperative and team-oriented approach to his fellow-workers. However, not everyone co-operated, and, at times, he addressed those who departed from the teaching received from the Lord.

Summary:

1. Comparing contributions to failure evidence common experiences among Biblical and modern servants of God.
2. Understanding the effect of stress in failure is crucial.
3. Burnout commonly precedes failure.
4. Differentiating between failure and sin is important to understanding.
5. Sin is both personal and corporate and may have its origin both from within and from outside influences.
6. Ministry is in the context of imperfection.

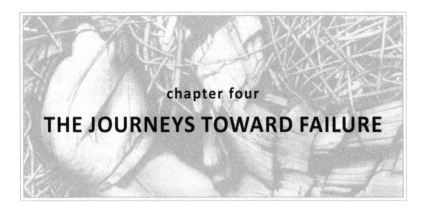

chapter four
THE JOURNEYS TOWARD FAILURE

I f we employ the analogy of a journey that leads to the destination called failure, we can address the issue in this manner. To make our analogy more concrete, let us assume you are taking a journey from Toronto to North Bay. The route is quite direct if we take highway number 400 North, joining number 11 and continuing to North Bay. According to Google Maps, the distance is 357 kilometers and would take 3 hours and 33 minutes. As anyone who knows this area of Ontario will know, you must past pass by or through many places on the way, including Barrie, Orillia, Gravenhurst, Huntsville, Sundridge, South River and many other smaller locations.

In other words, there are many places where you might turn off the scheduled journey. In any case, if you decided or was assisted to decide to discontinue the journey, you would not arrive at North Bay. Similarly, in the "unchosen" journey toward failure, there are many places along the way where "re-routing," termination, or any form of discontinuation of the journey would mean that you would not arrive at the destination of failure.

I have had opportunity to be engaged with thousands of individuals in ministry. I have witnessed many broken boughs who were formerly very fruitful. Thus, as a professional counsellor who has walked alongside many after they have journeyed to failure, I am convinced that interventions earlier in the process would have led to the avoidance of failure as an outcome.

My perspective has been retrospective, going back to the family of origin dynamics, the educational experience, the theological training, identifying the expectations of the individual upon entering ministry, the awakening to the realities of the experiences in ministry, and the accumulations of the pressures of his or her ministry. There is considerable consistency, once the journey has begun, as to the relational, emotional, spiritual, physical and family aspects of an experience that leads to failure. These are five quite identifiable journeys that constitute the progress toward the destination of failure. Without assistance, these are usually not defined by the pastor. They were unchosen destinations.

An Unchosen Destination

Failure is not a chosen destination. No one enters ministry with the intent to fail, nor to falter. Most express their desire to finish strong. However, failure is the outcome for many.[194] We may explain this outcome in a variety of ways. When it happens in a church context, it is usually addressed as a moral problem. Sometimes, it will be explained as financial inability to pay for pastoral services,[195] as a failure to experience church growth, a result of changing demographics, or incompatible differences. These are not chosen outcomes. Pastors do not plan to fail.

To understand failure, we must look at the journeys that led down that pathway. If, in response to the incident of failure, we focus only on judging the incident we will not achieve understanding. It is a severe limitation to fail to understand the contributing factors. Since the outcome was neither planned nor anticipated, we must seek an understanding as to what led up to it. What preceded this outcome? Could it have been foreseen? What were the factors that contributed to it? Was it solely what was going on in the life of the pastor? What contribution did the church leadership or membership make? Were there factors outside of the church that shared the responsibility for what happened? Different kinds of failure are the outcome of different processes. Yet, there are common elements present along the journey in most experiences of failure.

A Multifaceted Journey

Indeed, the journey toward failure is a journey with multiple facets. We might best describe it as multiple journeys that are occurring with synchronicity. Synchronicity means that several things are functioning in a rhythm of relationship. The various factors are contributing in their own way, adding to the whole of the experience.

In an orchestra, there are many instruments, each contributing its own part in a way that accomplishes the presentation of the whole musical composition. A painting is created from distinct colors being added, blended, and contrasted with various shapes incorporated as they create the whole painting. The finished product does not suddenly appear.

In failure, there are several journeys occurring in sync, each contributing its part. At any point, one will take precedence over the others—but in harmony, each impacting the others. At a conscious level, we will be aware of the more predominant contributions. The subtler elements may be just below the level of our awareness but will play a major role in the background.

To understand the whole, we must honor and understand the contribution of each part. There are five journeys occurring in an interactive fashion. Sometimes in an individual these journeys will be clashing or buffeting one another for attention or supremacy. The five journeys are:

1.The Relational Journey
2.The Emotional Journey
3.The Spiritual Journey
4.The Physical Journey
5.The Family Journey

Figure 5

The Five Contributing Journeys

The Relational Journey

The relational journey toward failure was different for each of the seven people in our stories. We will look briefly, and in summary fashion, at each of the journeys of Jim, Mel, and Jordon. In retrospect, we were able to assess the development of their relational isolation, and better grasp its impact on them and the outcome of their ministry.

Jim's experience and expectations in relationships were deeply imbedded in his family of origin. His family was close, interdependent, openly honest with each other, and very generous to all with whom they related in their community. Thus, Jim became very extroverted, socially engaged, and wishing to be involved in his community and his congregation. It took him sometime to grasp that the underlying tensions within his board, and the deception and dishonesty represented, was disquieting to him in his spirit. It was like the rumbling of tectonic plates below the surface of the earth. Eruption was a feared possibility. Eventually, he was disillusioned by the rosy picture presented. The strong and unrelenting undercurrents made every decision an experience of walking on egg shells. He lost trust in the church leadership. Gradually this increased to cynicism.

The double message he received about his involvement with the community was confusing. On the one hand, he was encouraged to be involved because it was good for the church. On the other hand, he was cautioned about engagement with "the world." The legalism and strong separatist focus of some of the key families left him unsettled. It wasn't explicit but clearly his style of engagement was questionable. He was also confused about the board's desire for prominence in the community, yet they feared of engagement with the community. He didn't know for sure if he was doing what the leadership wanted. He was confused.

He withdrew from any close relationship with the board because of this confusion. He justified that as his need to put more time in congregational care. The addition of an associate, although it promised relief, just increased his work load. He had no time for managing a team and, anyway, they seemed to want to be independent. There was little support from that quarter.

The greatest relational loss was with Sally. The growing needs of the children, coupled with a very inadequate income, required her to work long hours. She just could not be there for him. This was a total reversal of the expectations he had brought from his family of origin. They had provided strength for each other, loyalty, interaction, humor, and unconditional acceptance. He lost all of that.

He dug deeper into his work at the church. Going home meant unmet expectations. Sally was always exhausted. The children felt they didn't have what their friends had. He began to experience his home as a place of failure. Failure at home, along with the confusion and failure at church to find supportive relationships, drove him to deepening self-negation and, soon, depression. He was not measuring up to anyone's expectations and probably not God's either. Loneliness became a constant undercurrent in his brooding and rumination. Driven into isolation, Jim turned in the absence of an experience of nurturing in his relational community to self-nurture and self-comfort in soft pornography. Loss of community often leads to self-indulgence.

There were similarities and differences in Mel's experience. He, too, was an extrovert. From youth, he was expected to lead and did so with great success. A major reason for this was the constant and deserved affirmation and encouragement he received from so many others. In ministry, he discovered, in retrospect, that success is not victory. Indeed, success brought overwhelming demands of relational involvement on the one hand and isolation of the other.

Mel thrived on the demands of involvement with people when he was ministering to them. However, when they demanded supervision, rightly deserved, he found that was a different kind of demand. When the team grew to the place where his relational role changed to supervision, management, negotiation of limited resources, the discipline of requiring accountability from subordinates, Mel was out of his depth. The apportioning of limited resources among competing demands was a new chore. And indeed, a chore it was. A group of high-powered, committed specialists seeking to do their best challenged his skills. The loudness of demands from every direction led to him retreating from this exposure to the clanging sound of great expectations. He felt like a business man I met who declared, "All people want from me is my money or my problem-solving skills. They have no interest in me."

There was no time to create the collegiality of a team, nor the knowledge of how to create one. He was told that he was responsible for the whole of the ministry but did not have the relational resources to bring such a diverse group together. Corporate strategizing incentives didn't work in what was essentially a volunteer organization.

The loneliness of the spotlight, required for camera perfection in presenting his Sunday sermon, isolated him from visual engagement with his audience. He could no longer see the responsiveness in the faces of those to whom he ministered. Besides, he never saw or got to know the people in satellite churches. To many of them he was just a voice, a celebrity with no personal contact. He seemed to be ministering to people with whom he had no relationship. In some way, it seemed like acting. The orchestration of every detail reduced the reality. Under the pressure to perform, he lost the creativity, spontaneity, and personal relationships with those he loved.

Mel was experiencing relational poverty. That was increased by the anger that boiled over from his frustration with the demands. His relational explosion with staff and board accumulated to large proportions. Long days, sleepless nights with an unhappy wife, and children wanting more of their dad, led to his further retreat into self. Circling within the small space of self-imposed isolation, he became vulnerable. He needed someone to care, to help him to carry a burden that had become too heavy. His previous joyful reaching out to people evaporated. He was left alone. The man who had wanted to be a servant of others became a celebrity in a crowd where no one really knew or cared for him.

Jordon's relational journey began in a very different place. His family lived in relative poverty. They were, however, mostly unaware of that reality. They didn't have much but much of what they had was given away to others they deemed to be in greater need. The family clung to each other with tenacity and support. They served relatives and friends alike in compassion and care. They were known as "rocks" in the community, people who could be counted on. They gave to others until it hurt but instead of experiencing hurt, they had a sense of joy in giving. All they needed to do was work harder and their faith would carry them through. Life was defined by his caring family and their service to others expressed their Christian faith. This was a wonderful gift that Jordon soaked up from the model his family provided.

In college, he discovered counselling as a vehicle for expressing care. Although the training was minimal, it was inspiring. Life became defined by caring relationships. Caring and counselling became hallmark in the community.

However, he soon became consumed by the overwhelming needs of others. Social and justice issues became his focus. In caring for others, he forgot to care for himself. Neither the senior pastor nor leadership in the church saw his need for care. They did not understand his passion or the over-extension it created. When he sought support and was rejected, he turned inward. Feeling abandoned to his personal calling, he withdrew further into being consumed by compassion. Using his own limited resources, he fell deeper into a lonely depression drowning in the needs of others.

The Emotional Journey

In our culture, emotions have come to the forefront. At other times in history, emotions were not given such a high priority. Emotions are often thought of as feelings. The feelings are an outcome of what is happening in the body. The central core of the brain, usually defined as the "emotional brain,"[196] is made up of two parts. This is the source of much of what we experience as emotion. One of its roles is essentially a protective one. It warns of impending danger by activating the body's stress response system. When triggered by any sense of concern, fear or alarm, it releases a cascade of stress hormones and nerve impulses that drive up our blood pressure, heart rate, breathing, etc. This prepares the body for action. Even a minimal concern begins the process, though we are not immediately conscious of this process in our bodies. The reason is that the emotional brain (sometimes referred to as the low road) responds immediately, prior to our awareness.

The awareness occurs in another part of the brain, often referred to as the rational brain. The rational brain processes experience. However, it is slower in response than the emotional brain. This leads to action before thinking. Thus, awareness of one's body becomes a key factor in early detection of minimal distress or concern. Our emotional response is physiological. Slowing down the reactive outcome provides time for cognitive understanding or assessment to occur. We are very conscious of these effects when they reach the level of high emotion as in anger, fear, fright or rage.

In the Hebrew Scriptures, one of the words translated "anger" contains the imagery of a "burning stomach," which we have all experienced.[197] We now understand what is going on in the body when this happens. When the stress response reaches a certain level, we are all aware of a heavy heart beat. Many of the subtle responses of the body are just as real and have their effect, even if they occur outside of our awareness.

The triggering of these effects is related very much to past experiences going back to childhood. In people suffering from PTSD, the speed and severity of these responses are obvious. If one is under minimal stress over time this will result in a chronic condition and the continuation of this aroused state.

Understanding the physiology of emotion becomes crucial in grasping what a pastor is experiencing in his emotional journey toward failure. When emotional responses accumulate, they inhibit the regulatory system as well as lowering the effectiveness of the immune system.

A pastor's experience of emotion due to frustration about leadership, such as a sense of not fulfilling expectations, of breaching of his values related to his definition, of success in ministry or family responsibility, or the emotional exhaustion of overload, accumulate in their effect. They become a patterned response that triggers the same pattern to occur more quickly and strongly. They escalate from frustration to anger, depression, self-doubt, a sense of hopelessness and despair. The more these responses are experienced, the more they impact our perception of our world. Thinking is confused until we reach the state of Macbeth,"

Oh horror! Horror! Horror! Tongue nor heart cannot conceive nor name thee! Confusion now hath made his masterpiece!"[198]

This process is adequately illustrated in the experience of Jim, Mel and Jordon. Consider Jim's experience. Early on, he became aware, at a minimal level, of the tensions in the board. The subtlety and burial of the differences under a code of silence confused him at first. As his ministry progressed, he became more aware of the deception and dishonesty. He had not experienced this while growing up. Added to that, he was caught between the pressure for community involvement, on the one hand, and the anxiety of the "legalistic" element in the church that seemed concerned that they should be "separate from the world" on the other. The squeeze increased over time. He felt emotionally torn. He came to feel that he was not honored by several of the board members. He came to feel less attached to the leadership and began to resent board meetings. The micro-management of the board added pressure.

Other pressures mounted. The expectation to supervise the associate who was hired increased the pressure. He had less time to fulfill his social needs in community relationships. The strain of financial pressure increased as his family grew. The necessity of his wife generating income led to them losing mutual support of each other. The sense of being abandoned, on the one hand,

and being the center piece of success, on the other, increased his feelings of failure.

These various pieces of his experience generated much emotional reactivity. He withdrew more and more into his own world of brooding and loneliness. Eventually, his emotional response became evidenced in cynicism, anger, sarcasm and more emotional distance from those whom he needed care. He was experiencing emotions he had never learned to cope with. A sense of inadequacy increased. Lacking care from others, he turned to self-care, self-nurture and, eventually, the world of fantasy. His emotional life absorbed his interest and he lost control. The depth of his loss of a sense of belonging and attachment to his board is evidenced in his refusal to share with them his reason for his resignation.

The emotional journey of Mel and Jordon had both similar and different elements than that of Jim's.

The Spiritual Journey

The spiritual and emotional are entwined in the consciousness of most people causing these two to become almost inseparable. However, it is possible to separate them and, in the therapeutic relationship, necessary to do so. In the previous section, the chemical/neurological aspects of emotions were touched on briefly. Our emotional response begins in the brain and pervades the entire body. Our interpretation of those internal activities is a cognitive process. Emotions begin first, and then rational explanation tries to make sense of the experience. The rationalization impacts the spiritual understanding of experience. Thus, spiritual experience is inextricably bound to emotional experience.

It is painful to retrace with pastors the spiritual journey that they have experienced in their journey toward failure. There is much similarity from person to person.

Our spirituality is such a central part of our personal being that the spiritual responses along the journey to failure have much in common. The intensity of the spiritual battle increases as we move along that journey, which no one plans to take, toward the crisis that leads to the terminal experience. Perhaps, the best way to convey that is to quote for you a poem I wrote at the time I was walking that pathway with a very successful servant of God.[199]

I Listened to Pain

Portions of the past
Depressed, pushed down,
Stuffed deep,
Sealed in silence.
Pain pushed to oblivion.

Yet, bubbling, boiling,
Building pressure,
Crouching to spring,
Disguised in a confusion
Of distorted emotions.

Yet, nowhere to turn but inward.
Steel-cold eyes unfocused
In tight intensity, while thoughts
Repeating patterns of self-blame,
Self-hate undeserved but unavoidable.

Anger screamed in silence
Shattering the body
With tremors of emotion.
Body friend becomes body enemy.

Pain shouted silently
Through body language in vain trembling,
Clenched fists, thin lips, knotted stomach.
Eyes crying dry tears
Burning with unblinking stares.

Spiritual pain permeates the entire body. What we cannot put into words, our bodies express. Often, we do not interpret the body language as spiritual pain, but the origin is often there, deeply imbedded in the soul. The spiritual coolness creeps silently into the crevices of the inner being. Feelings, not seen as spiritual crying, sweep through our neurological systems to express themselves, often disguised as discomfort, aches, unwellness and, if endured for long, in other more extreme expressions.

One can see the evidence of the relationship between the spiritual, emotional, relational, and physical in the lives of Elijah and David. The emotional exhaustion following Elijah's battle with the gods of Baal, immediately followed by all the running he did from King Ahaz and in fear of Jezebel, and, then, his race into the desert left him in a terrible state. It is not always easy to discern which comes first; the physical, spiritual or emotional fatigue. They become very mixed. Normally, when one is present, the others are not far away.

This was the case with Jim, Mel and Jordon. Each of these enemies of the soul creep surreptitiously into our consciousness. It begins with forgetting or loosening our spiritual disciplines. Then coolness sets in and guilt begins. We stop talking to God quite so much and negative emotions (partly determined by personality or habit) play a role. Eventually, we come to feel unloved, unappreciated, not understood, used, etc. These are like a creeping vine that eventually strangles what it encircles.

In my experience with pastors this process is virtually always a precursor to failure. Frequently, we may rationalize it as a "dark night of the soul" or we may interpret it as spiritual warfare. There is no question of Satan's involvement. It is his access point to our lives, and he celebrates the deterioration of spirituality and leads us on in what Jesus called Peter's "sifting." It would be very difficult to separate the emotional and spiritual agony of Peter in his failure. That is equally so in the cases of Elijah, David, Jim, Mel and Jordon.

In many ways our spiritual lives are cradled by our emotions. This is not to deny the role of our wills, which would be illustrated in the lives of Jonah or Daniel. The training of the will and the rational affirmation of belief is not apart from faith or grace.

One of the central issues on the journey to failure is the inhibition of our rational function amid emotional, spiritual and relational confusion. Both the clarity of our understanding and commitment to our knowledge of God plays a key role in our emotional and spiritual experience. This is also greatly impacted by our experience of community as relational beings.

The Physical Journey

Some years ago, returning home from a long and arduous experience of ministry overseas, I visited my doctor to complain of extreme itching on my legs, which was becoming unbearable. He began by asking about my latest trips abroad (he knew this was a frequent occurrence). I explained briefly, if somewhat impatiently, as I wanted attention to my legs. He casually examined my condition and observed, "In your case, the body weeps for one who does not know how to weep for himself!" My response was not sensitive. "What has that to do with my legs?" He explained that the stress I had endured expressed itself in one of my weaker systems, i.e. my very sensitive skin.

We see a similar response in Elijah's experience and in that of Jim, Mel and Jordon. Quite literally, stress will come out. Where it manifests itself will depend on several variables. Our bodies are an integrated number of systems, such as the skin, our neurological system, the cardio-vascular system, our skeletal system, etc. Stress will speak through whichever of these systems is weakest or whichever is most closely related to the pressure we are experiencing. Those, who are stronger constitutionally, may endure stress that becomes more severe or lasts over a lengthier time. However, the body eventually expresses itself. As Dr. Van Der Kolk puts it, "The body keeps the score."[200] Experiences leave traces in the body. As these residues accumulate, they will find expression in

115

the body. He also points out that the lies we tell ourselves are the greatest sources of our suffering.

The journey often begins with weariness, which soon grows into exhaustion. Self-isolation leads to brooding, and then to rumination. Eventually, we begin to feel tired, then low, and then move into ill-defined discomfort in the stomach, back, shoulders, etc. We may produce flu-like symptoms. Most are not very clear, at first. Headaches are more common. Sleep disturbance increases. Hypertension, skeletal pain, ulcers and, eventually, heart disease suddenly hits. The appearance of these symptoms is determined by many things such as age, history, genetics, and other influences. We can be sure that the relational, spiritual, emotional, and physical journeys toward failure are integrated in mysterious interdependence.

Let me mention again that the focus on the terminal point of the journey unfortunately leads us to fail in recognizing the many elements that contribute to the outcome. Our preoccupation with the moral or dramatic nature of the "straw that broke the camel's back" leads us to overlook the potential for intervention and course correction as we move toward failure. The terminal point would very likely not have occurred if we had been aware of the many contributing factors along the way. Each dimension of the journey toward failure requires us to understand the differing responses of each person. If not, our minds readily confuse or misdirect us to what are symptoms and we may not connect all the dots. The body does not. The body keeps score.

The Family Journey

Ministry is a family affair. Historically, the expectations of the family members' involvement in the ministry of the pastor have varied greatly. The range has been from a total non-involvement to the expectation that in hiring a pastor the church is getting two in ministry for the price of one through his wife's or children's involvement. I do not wish to engage in what is good, better, or best. There is much that is personal in that decision and it is determined greatly by the culture in which the church is located, economic demands and the needs or expectations, and the parent/child relationship. The commitment of some to home schooling will place certain expectations on the family, as will the expectations of a certain style of living.

In the interest of full disclosure, I would simply indicate that the principle, which guided the decisions of my wife and I, was that one of us should not expose ourselves to what could be a life changing event without the other being part of it. Apart from a few weeks of research in a psychiatric hospital in Scotland in 1968, my wife has travelled with me in ministry to many countries of the world. When our children were in their young teens, we felt it necessary to take them with us overseas for an extended time of ministry. My ministry in difficult situations was greatly enhanced by the presence of both my wife and children. I do not consider my experience a pattern for the calling of others. However, walking along the journey with many others in ministry, it has become evident to me that ministry significantly impacts family experience and that of the pastor's ministry in reciprocal fashion.

The illustrations from Scripture present a mixed picture. We remember the relationship between Adam and Eve. She was to be a helper but appeared to take the lead in yielding to Satan's temptation.[201] Certainly, Sarah's beauty, her guidance to Abraham's relationship to Hagar, and her laughing at God's promise impacted Abraham in his relationship with Jehovah.[202] Also, Job's wife's urging of him to *"curse God and die"* and Job's rebuttal that she was "talking like a foolish woman," illustrates the point that spouses may have strong influences.[203] It is not easy to understand God's command to Hosea, the prophet, that he should, *"Go take to yourself an adulterous wife and children of unfaithfulness."*[204] Paul was very explicit in stating his preference for singleness while honoring the Lord's brothers and Cephas in taking their wives with them in ministry.[205]

The issues that arise from the normal tensions by the presence of children in families are many. These illustrations may shoe that we should be aware, and carefully take into consideration, the realities of both the enormous contribution and the liabilities associated with marriage and family when ministry is the call upon one's life.

As Jim and Mel explored how their families related to their journey, it became evident that their engagement in ministry impacted their involvement in the family. Also, their family added other pressures that contributed to their experience.

Of course, Jordon is an example of a single person in ministry. Jordon's family modeled compassion in the context of relative poverty. His family became a model of rescuing others. They were very supportive of each other and very hard-working. As a single person away from a supportive home, he had no awareness of what he was really missing.

Jim's experience of family in his family of origin played a significant role in the setting of his expectations for his relationship with Sally. A tight-knit farm family, with a high level of engagement and support during personal struggles and a deep commitment to meet the needs of others, would summarize Jim's experience. His experience began with ideals of relationship which included mutual support, intimacy, frequent communication, and a sense of team-work in ministry. These ideals were shattered by the necessity of Sally finding work to make ends meet financially. When the children came along, their time together was further compromised. Sally's increasing health issues added another major level of pressure. They drifted, essentially without conflict, into dark places of isolation from each other. There was no anger but just a dogged determination to respond to the needs of others and the children, without any awareness of the need to reflect on their experience. Survival became the name of the game. They assumed that suffering was one of the costs of ministry. They rather passively accepted what was dealt to them. Disappointment occupied the space that had formerly been filled with intimacy and support. Really, Jim's final panic and rush back into Sally's arms felt like a gain and a recovery. Thus, they clung to each other, unwilling to address the issues at the church. They knew they were running away but, at least, they were running together. It seemed to them they had gone in a circle; first into darkness but back to the light of each other's commitment.

Mel's family journey was quite different. They were upper middle class with few concerns and a provided a very happy, supportive environment. His family was dynamic, assertive, and successful. Mel knew what it was like to be successful and he enjoyed the experience. Both he and Millie were strong individuals. In some ways, they responded similarly to their challenges. As Mel's challenges continued to exceed his capacity, he became frustrated. This eventually heightened to where he could acknowledge and name his experience as anger. The evidence was very explicit. His response to demands in ministry took him away from both Millie and his growing family. Ministry success was more important. Deterioration in his relationship with Millie was responded to by her with challenges and accusations which Mel personalized. She was strong enough to be confrontational in their relationship and frequently nursed her anger, planning ways to confront or challenge Mel about his abandonment of the children and his absorption in his high-profile role. Mel could not deal with her response and so retreated further into the needs of ministry. Longer hours increased his separation from Millie and the anger of the children toward a demanding church and a dad who wasn't around. They learned to express their feelings as they witnessed the emotional expression on the part of their parents. They reflected what they saw. Millie had tried to be a buffer between the children and their dad but had not succeeded in hiding her real feelings. She had insight into what was happening but no words with which to articulate her observations to Mel. When Mel came home and confessed, she rose to the occasion with an ultimatum that expressed her anger, her commitment, and a plan to move forward. She used her power to insist that part of moving forward was receiving professional help. Her insistence led them to recovery as a family, but the issues in the church were not addressed. Their denomination had no room for moral failures, so they moved on—unconnected and disillusioned for some time.

Harmony and Discord in the Journeys

The way in which each journey is managed is different for everyone. Each conductor of an orchestra will creatively use the range of instruments and the skills of each musician in unique manner. So, each person will have a different level of awareness of what element of his experience will receive focus. Some are very aware of relational tensions; some will focus on family or physical discomfort. Each will respond uniquely.

The art of seeking an understanding of each person's experience begins with whatever the person is most aware of and leading them to explore the role of each contributing factor. As with an orchestra, the whole is composed of the many parts. In reflection, the discord or competing interests of each part becomes clear. Then, one must explore the role of the church, the leadership, the members of the congregation, cultural input, denominational expectations and any other contributing factors, which in concert, contributed toward the conclusion of the journey. From this perspective, I expect it is evident how necessary it is to look at much more than the incident of failure.

The important work may be just beginning. As indicated earlier, the incident must be dealt with in a biblical manner. The pastor will need to come to understand how confession, repentance, restoration, restitution, and the spiritual renewal are all necessary. This will include dealing with the family impact. However, we must also consider restoration of fellowship and, where appropriate, re-engagement in ministry. Dealing with these issues require a lengthier discussion between the pastor and counselor. Next, we will discuss the matter of intervention prior to the incident of failure.

Summary:

1. Failure is an unchosen, unplanned pathway in ministry.
2. There are five different journeys that combine to lead to that undesired destination.

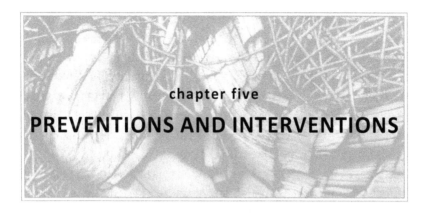

PREVENTIONS AND INTERVENTIONS

DURING THE PAST 50 YEARS AS I HAVE HAD OPPORTUNITY TO BE engaged with thousands of individuals in ministry, I have witnessed many who have become broken who were formerly very fruitful. After failure, I have walked with them through the journey that led to that destination. We explored their experience along their life to that point. Most have learned much about what led to that destination. I am convinced that interventions earlier in the process would have led to avoiding failure. My perspective has been retrospective in going back to the family or origin dynamics, the educational experience, the theological training, identifying expectations upon entering ministry, the awakening to the realities of ministry, and the succumbing to the pressures of ministry. There is considerable consistency once the journey has begun as to the relational, emotional, family, spiritual, and physical aspects of the experience that leads to failure.

Interventions Along the Journey of Failure

Intervention early along the way would have terminated the journey before that destination of failure was reached. It is possible to identify those opportune times for intervention. There are a few basic requirements if that outcome is to be avoided. First the pastor must be an aware of the factors that may identify the beginning of the journey toward failure. Secondly, he must be open and vulnerable enough to enable the identification of early symptoms. Thirdly, a safe place where early evidence can be explored is required. It is obvious that all of these require awareness, openness, and sensitivity to one's personal experience and a willingness to receive assistance. The first two of these require a capacity for self-awareness. The second is facilitated by an openness for mentoring and/or supervision by someone who can provide a safe place for such exploration. In these many ways, the pastor is the key. However, he needs others who can be sensitively present in his life.

However, the pastor is not alone in this experience. He is part of a church or other Christian community and, usually, a denomination or mission organization. There is much that others within the pastor's faith community can do. Boards of elders or deacons, church members who are observant, denominational leaders, and other pastors have a definite role to play. Structures of accountability, such as Paul experienced in his team in New Testament times, are needed in churches and denominations. We must grasp the fact that pastors do not stand or fall alone.

Biblical Models of Interventions

The New Testament is rich with a wealth of information as to the interdependence of the churches. Also, the engagement by Paul of many to work with him in leading the churches to a place where they appropriately represented the life of Jesus in their relationships is very clear. The itinerant work of all the Apostles, in as much as we know about that, evidences a similar care among the churches. The evidence indicates that the Apostles, who were dispersed through the known world, nurtured churches and mentored the elders/pastors and other church leadership in both the acceptable Christian patterns and in how to live in the world without compromising the faith.

The Apostle Paul & Interventions

The Apostle Paul illustrates this. His epistles are full of encouragement, affirmation, counsel, guidance, accountability, confrontations, and prayer for his fellow-workers. He was overwhelmingly aware of his fellow-citizens, joint-heirs, the joint-body, and joint-sharers who participated with him in the promises in Christ.[206] These words of participation with each other in Christ are worthy of detailed study. However, in the same vein, Paul was aware of his relationship with those engaged with him in ministry. He lists at least fifteen by name and refers to others. They are described as brothers, partners, labourers, soldiers, prisoners, and yoke-fellows bound together as a team. To translate Paul's words, we would need to use hyphenated words like fellow-worker. The emphases are on their being joined inseparably in the task.[207] The interdependence, peer ministry, and mutual support of those engaged in ministry is profound in its depth and supportive engagement. The current use of ministries such as mentoring, coaching, peer counselling or other types of support groups may represent the relationship Paul maintained with his fellow-servants.

It was not simply Paul ministering to those he worked with. Paul urgently needed support when he found himself in deep depression and despair in Macedonia. God came alongside of him in the person of Titus.[208] Titus had been ministered to by the church in Corinth and, in turn, ministered to Paul. This is the model for peer support and nurturing that can rescue pastors who are on the journey toward failure. Without a doubt in Paul's understanding of ministry, the little word "with" is most powerful when linked, as he does, with other words of action and intervention.

We must grasp the power of presence to comprehend the meaning. It is being with another in depth—accepting, seeking joint outcomes, common goals with action, support, clarification, understanding, empathy, and love. It is being with another in trouble, trial, and warfare, and joining in the burden-bearing, burden-sharing, and mutual seeking of God the Deliverer.

Paul provides the language of intervention in his relationship with his fellow-servants. It is a rich and full language of mentoring and redemption. Learning from this, pastoral conferences could be designed to foster vulnerability, peer care, awareness, acknowledgement of need, respite from the pressures of ministry, and opportunities of renewal. This may require a shift from using conferences and conventions to stimulate greater efforts, greater growth, more profound preaching, and other such things to a focus on care and nurture of pastors. This would help pastors to shift from the disciples' distraction of competition to pastors nurturing pastors.

We need to be clear about another issue. From a medical perspective, there is not much value in increasing the awareness and sensitivity of a patient to any early symptoms of a disease if there is no doctor with whom they can consult about early intervention. This applies to pastors. If pastors, through their theological training or denominational instruction, developed a sensitivity to the early signs of issues that could lead to failure, we would then need to have opportunities in place for them where they can consult with others who have the experience and sensitivity to provide a safe place for that to occur. Issues of confidentiality would need to be addressed. Also, a clear understanding of the role of those providing this ministry to denominational leadership would require clarity. Training for those in such a role is the responsibility of the denomination as is the need to make this financially possible.

Let me quickly add that the intervention would not likely require the expertise of a professional counsellor. Intervening at the early stages of prevention could be adequately handled by peer care, church care, family care and personal care. This would necessitate the peer responder being adequately trained for that response of comfort, admonition, edification, strengthening and nurture. You will note that all these interventions are Biblically prescribed methods of helping believers toward maturity and growth in Christ.

Abraham's Experience

Let's look back to Abraham's experience. As limited as we are in knowing details, we can draw some lessons from what we glean form the biblical account. It is safe to assume Abraham expected God's blessing in response to his obedience to the call. He placed himself in God's hands. His faith carried him from Haran to Canaan, but this was a land full of enemies. He encountered the Canaanites, thinking he had the resources to deal with them. Famine was not what Abraham expected. Going from the plenty of Mesopotamia to the potential of perishing in Canaan was challenging. From feasting to famine is a frightening step. Famine evolved into fear. Was this all a mistake? The threat of death is a powerful motivator. His heart was "failing him from fear."

Today, we know fear evolves into anger, heart attacks, migraines, and depression. Abraham created a plan when what he needed was faith. He was a man of action. He decided to go where there was food. He went to Egypt, a place of plenty much like the familiar delta of Mesopotamia. Possibly, fear drove him to seek the familiar rather than the ambiguity of faith. Fear-based behaviour usually leads to a different path than faith-based behaviour. Maybe there is a clue in his son's experience, when God said, "Don't go down into Egypt."[209] Maybe if Abraham had consulted God, he would have received the same advice. Abraham's lie resulted in him acquiring a great deal of prosperity from Pharaoh, but it was costly to Pharaoh. Sometimes the cost of sin in the leadership is costly to those around the sinner. The plagues were horrible. Pharaoh heard God, confronted Abraham, and chased him out of the country.

When Abraham succumbed to Sarah's suggestion to have a child by Hagar, he submitted once again to seeking a humanly-designed solution. Often people are encouraged into sin by the enabling of others. Sarah was trapped in her pain of infertility. Impatience often drives us to desperation. Faith is laid aside in the interest of clutching our own solutions. Rationalizing our way into trouble is not unusual. Submission to faithless suggestions scuttles faith and leads to laughing at God's promises. It was not so much Abraham's lack of faith as Sarah's fear of failure to deliver an heir that lead to this faltering of confidence in God's ability to do what he said he would do. Partnership in sin is still sin. The resultant pain was great.

Could there have been a different outcome if intervention had occurred in either of these situations? Consulting God or seeking consensus with his family may have saved Abraham the grief and failure of Egypt. The dynamic of the spousal relationship between Abraham and Sarah could have been different. Could Abraham have been a stronger leader in his family? The answer is, "Yes." Indeed, we know that God in his sovereignty worked things according to his will. But we can learn that fear, the influence of others closest to us, and leadership issues can play a large role in our journey. These three factors play a significant part in moving pastors along the journey toward failure.

Elijah's Experience

Elijah is an example of burnout. James[210] tells us Elijah prayed for drought and it did not rain for three years. During that time, he was fed by ravens, multiplied food for the widow of Zarephath, raised her son to life, and then, at God's instruction, went to confront King Ahab. He used a mediator, Obadiah by name, who informed him he had hidden one hundred prophets of God from the King. Ahab responded to Elijah's invitation, which led to the confrontation with the Baal prophets. He then commanded the King to eat and drink because he was about to pray for rain. He climbed Mount Carmel and earnestly prayed. The exhaustion from all this activity, not withstanding, he ran ahead of Ahab all the way to Jezreel in the South of Judah, a very long way by foot from Carmel. The message of his impending death at the instigation of Jezebel sent him into terror and fear. Afraid for his life he ran to Beersheba, left his servant, and went on alone a day's journey into the desert where he collapsed in depression. Renewed with food by an angel and strengthened thereby, he travelled forty days and nights to Horeb where he was confronted by the Lord.

God intervened. God's intervention was necessary because Elijah had isolated himself. Irrationality replaced faith. Obadiah had told Elijah about the one hundred prophets he had saved. However, both in talking to the King and to the Lord, he declared he was the only faithful one remaining. After the "gentle whisper" from the Lord, he declared his zeal, his disappointment in Israel's unfaithfulness and his fear of being killed. Even the work of Obadiah was eclipsed by God's knowledge of seven thousand faithful whom God had reserved.

Exhaustion, isolation, loneliness, fear of enemies— visible and invisible; real and imagined—are part of the journey toward failure. The sense of being alone in faithfulness and ministry, physical exertion beyond reason and inadequate physical care of one's self are all evidences that the journey toward failure has begun. God intervened by bringing him an associate, Elisha. This, it would seem, by placing him on a pedestal which added expectations. Thus, even "his attendant"[211] added pressure to his experience. He knew himself to be "a man of God"[212] able to call down fire from heaven, but being "he was a human being, even as we are,"[213] he broke under the pressure of ministry in the same manner as servants of God today.

David's Experience

What can we say about David? Can we imagine his experience in growing up as the youngest and least in his family assigned and being assigned the lowliest task? Providentially, he came to know the faithfulness of God and developed great prowess in protecting the family's sheep. In faithfully fulfilling this task he probably honed his skills in musical and poetic expression. He acquired a level of skill so that later he was called upon to use his gifts in therapeutic ministry to King Saul. His relational sensitivity was manifest in his relationship with Jonathan and his leadership of the rabble that followed him when he was hounded by Saul.

What accumulated stress did he carry imbedded in his soul when finally crowned after he went out to war with the Jebusites, the Philistines and the Ammonites? He returned the Ark to Jerusalem but became very angry with God when Uzzah was killed for touching the ark as the oxen stumbled. He was mocked by Saul's daughter for celebrating with joy. But God assured David, through Nathan the prophet, that he would establish his kingdom and his successor would never be removed from God's love. He continued winning victory upon victory in war. He honoured Saul's family.

Then one time as was the custom at that time of the year the kings went out to war. David stayed at home. We are given no clear reason, but it was certainly unusual. In his leisure, he rose from his bed to walk in the cool of the evening on the roof top. There he saw a beautiful woman. He unwisely sent for her and she came. Who was the predator and who was the victim? Was it common for women to expose themselves while bathing? I can only say that when pastors fall into sensual response to nudity or provocative behaviour by women, it is not always clear who is the predator. We cannot fully grasp David's family of origin dynamics, the stress of being a fugitive, a warrior, a leader of great fighters, or the pressure of his kingship. We only know that these experiences led to unintentional, destructive behaviour. Moral failure correlates with the outcomes of such experiences.

Peter's Experience

Peter received his name from Christ who saw in him strength and resolve. Yet, the competitiveness among the disciples gave rise to Peter's pursuit of first place among them. On the other hand, he was first to declare Jesus as the Christ, the first to venture walking on the water, the one willing to obey in casting nets that had brought nothing in the night, the first to promise faithfulness to the death, the first to draw a sword in defence of Christ at his arrest, and the one of the two to follow Jesus to the trial. We know he was being "sifted" by Satan. The pressure that overwhelmed him by the fire was social but also, he feared the consequences of his relationship with Jesus. He had been reprimanded so often for his forwardness and now, by the fire, he was challenged by Roman authority that he feared. Emotionally, it is not difficult to understand his total disillusionment and sense of betrayal by Christ and by his fellow disciples. It is not a great leap to think he felt betrayed by Jesus' yielding himself so readily. And, where were the other disciples? He was alone, mentally naked, and ashamed at what was happening. Emotionally distraught, physically exhausted, and overwhelmed with grief, he denied knowing Jesus. His depth of despair was only deepened by his denial. His emotions plunged to the bottom as he heard the condemning voice of the rooster, reminding him of Jesus' words.

As difficult as it is with our paucity of information, we can at least in minimal way enter the experience of these men of faith who were so fruitful, but then broke under the burden of their experience. We cannot write off their fruitfulness. Can we see their failure with understanding, empathy and compassion? How would we fare in their situation? Surely, we must seek by God's wisdom to identify with them in understanding and grace. The reality that God did not abandon them surely should give us pause to seek understanding and to humbly learn from their experience.

A Negative Example

The experience of Job provides an example of intervention. The most effective time of the intervention of Job's friends was the seven days that they remained silent. After that helpful silence they launched into a constant adversarial interaction with Job that was accusative and judgmental. As is most frequently the case, an adversarial approach leads to a reactive response from the person accused. The person reacting in this manner is often, at some level aware of their guilt, but feel it necessary to defend against what they are interpreting as an attack on their integrity. Job's friends were found by God to have responded inappropriately. It is not difficult to imagine what David's response may have been if Nathan had not begun with a story to bring to the surface of his awareness David's values. Confrontation that begins with accusation often has the same outcome.

Modern Pastors and Intervention

If we study the five-fold journeys of these three individuals, Jim, Mel and Jordon, we can readily see the differences in their journey toward failure. It is important to see the differences as we address whether appropriate, timely interventions may have diverted them from failure. Having traveled, retrospectively, on these journeys with many in ministry and having addressed, in counselling, the many contributing factors, it is clear to me that early intervention would have averted the outcome of failure. The destination was not intentional or chosen but the accumulation of contributors moved, sometimes imperceptibly but unremittingly, toward failure.

Prevention is all about intervening as early in the journey as possible. Many of the accumulating factors could have been addressed effectively early in the process. In addressing these, I can be much more explicit than in dealing with the Biblical persons since I have travelled with many and have seen resolution. Tragically, the intervention was after the failure, discipline, brokenness, and after the impact of the tsunami waves of failure rushed through their families, churches and communities. It is necessary to identify where early intervention may have occurred.

It may surprise you to know the primary question fruitful people, who have failed, ask while engaged in professional counselling. Perhaps a concrete illustration would help. A full-time female Christian worker in a church, along with her spouse, were referred to me. The wife had been in a very responsible position which enabled the embezzlement of a large sum of money. My first question was, "How do you wish me to be of help to you?" The immediate response was, "Well, I know I did what I was accused of. What I need to know is why? What led me to do this? Why after walking with Christ all these years could I fall into this situation?"

This individual went on to indicate they (husband and wife together) had confessed to the congregation and were resolved to repay the entire amount plus legal fees. They were not asking for guilt to be relieved. They wanted understanding. They had not, at that point, faced the legal ramifications. This response is most often the case. Frequently their focus is on how to take responsibility for all the damage that has resulted in the lives of so many others. Quite typically, they focus on the needs of others. But, urgently, the question is "Why?"

Earlier in Chapter 4, five journeys were identified as common to most journeys toward failure. Intervention in one of these by itself will not prevent the movement toward failure. It is obvious that immoral behaviour is not engaged for one single reason. Multiple factors contribute to every failure in our physical, mental, spiritual, familial, or emotional lives. This is evidenced in so many who come for counselling. There are usually some answers to "why" if we can set aside judgment long enough to look at the big picture. This does not set aside or excuse the immoral behaviour, which we will look at later, but it does potentially open the door for much learning and growth. The spiritual ramifications for all involved are immense. One group of elders, after three hours of trying to understand their pastor's failure, concluded that they were largely responsible for the expectations, overloading, and pressure they had placed on their pastor. They felt the need to repent and to apologize to the pastor and, after appropriate restoration, re-instated him.

One can readily see that there are many answers to the "why" question. My question is, "Could we have prevented this process or intervened early?" My experience is a resounding, "Yes!" Most countries, who are intent on protecting their populations, will create an early warning system. The important question is, "Can we prevent or intervene early so as to avoid the disaster that so frequently ends a fruitful ministry?" There are some significant requirements if prevention and/or intervention are to occur. Generally, we give inadequate attention to prevention. Nor do we create the conditions for intervention. We must look at these.

Prevention and Intervention Possibilities
Very briefly, there are many places at which both prevention and intervention would have been appropriate in each of these pastors'

lives. In considering prevention or intervention, it would be help-ful to go back to the identification of five journeys (see chapter 4) which were the experience of these pastors.[214] The entrance into a person's life who needs intervention requires care as one iden-tifies the point of entry. Example: In seeking to enter the lives of juvenile delinquents with whom I worked, I found that I could enter their lives through sports, scuba stories, hunting stories or involvement with them in any sport. Once having established re-lationship, it was then often possible to enter other areas of their lives where the real need existed. Similarly, with pastors, interven-tion may often have to be indirect such as Nathan demonstrated.

Often, pastors so deeply consumed by the greatest hurt are un-aware of lesser issues that may provide a more effective entry point into his life. Self-awareness, often today expressed as mindfulness, would have helped in their understanding of their own personal functioning in relationships. The input of their familial upbring-ings created personality and behavioral patterns and expectations.

The dynamics of pastor-elder relationships created stress. Jim's elder's board was deeply divided and experienced undercur-rents that he was unaware of at first and later ill-equipped to han-dle. Jordon was abandoned by his senior pastor and church lead-ership. Mel was simply encouraged to drive toward the success his elders desired. These pastors all lacked adequate leadership skills and knowledge to deal with the high-powered business men and their corporate style of getting things done.

Leadership and conflict management from a Biblical perspec-tive would have been preventive. These pastors experienced in-adequate training in these areas. They did not know the need for nor how to develop supportive relationships within their church-es or their teams. My observation is that they were unprepared to the extent of not knowing where to turn for answers. There was no preparation or intervention to enable them to deal with feelings that became overwhelming and led to self-incrimination. They turned inward because there was no opportunity provided or sought for peer relationships that could be supportive. Each expected to care for others but had not learned either the need for care nor where to turn to receive it. Pastors who experience failure have rarely experienced mentoring or significant peer support.

Mel felt from his "high profile" image and the isolation from the congregation left him lonely. Neither Jim nor Mel had any preparation or intervention that would have opened them to being able to explore the impact of ministry on their spousal or family relationships. Their retreat into self soon led to very negative results, rumination, guilt, and emotional despair. Awareness of one's emotional responses and one's physical bodily expressions are important. Such awareness can lead to intervention early on and can provide appropriate management of such stress.

It is not difficult to imagine that more adequate preparation, which provides realistic expectations, or interventions dealing with early points of questioning, guilt or frustration, could have prevented the outcome in the lives of these fruitful boughs. At this point, we need to look at the "how" of prevention and intervention.

Prevention, Care, and Early Intervention

The preceding chapters have demonstrated that many varied and coloured strands go into the creation of the tapestry of failure in ministry. The multiplicity, variety, strength, texture, colour, and other dimensions may overwhelm us when we seek to pursue understanding. The purpose in intervening after the journey has ended in failure is to unravel, through understanding, the various threads out of which the tapestry was created. This is a difficult process. But when understanding is achieved, then the experience can be rewoven by learning what the Spirit of God wishes to teach. This is the goal. The learning often enables one to create new pathways that do not lead to failure. Each individual experience must be honoured in its individuality. It is true that everyone is as different as snowflakes, but since each snowflake is common in its composition, so persons have much in common too.

Patterns of human behaviour are surprisingly consistent. Our similarities, both in biological make-up, in relational, and in emotional responses, make it possible for us to generalize and to enter each other's experience with understanding. There is little room for dogmatism but much room for understanding. The purpose of intervening early in the journey is to avoid failure by learning from early indications, and then reroute the ministry direction.

Thus, we are first seeking ways in which the outcome of failure can be prevented, secondly, looking at how to implement care along the career path of a pastor and, thirdly, to suggest interventions. Many give more attention to their cars and other such necessities than the care of pastors.

Care must be continuous along the career path of ministry. It will become readily obvious that I am not thinking of the type of intervention requiring what we would call in our culture "professional help." Instead, I am suggesting how people in our communities of faith can intervene, including how fellow-pastors can participate along the pastoral journey in both prevention and intervention. Most pastors, who complete their journey in failure, have paid little attention to their care, nor have others sought to provide care such as mentoring, coaching or supervision.

Preparation for Pastoral Ministry

The dramatic differences between what these three pastors experienced in their families and what they experienced in their church communities contributed much to their responses. Family, education, church preparation and other factors need to be addressed in preparing our future fruitful boughs. Much of this can be assessed through personality and ability assessment as part of the preparation for ministry. Additionally, these dynamics could be addressed in the educational preparation for ministry. Academic preparation is necessary, but inadequate, if it does not include and self-understanding of what everyone brings from one's family of origin.

The Family

Most of the stories I have shared, both Biblical and pastoral, illustrate the role of family in shaping the candidate for ministry. Life starts in families. Many people are encouraged or challenged to consider ministry by parents, relatives, or others in ministry whom they encounter in growing up. Some, in retrospect, learn they were fulfilling the dream of others who encouraged or pushed them toward ministry. Only after a painful fall do they explore that motivation for their own ministry. Maintaining a family dynasty in ministry or following another's dream may lead to questionable outcomes.

It is abundantly clear that values, self-understanding, the capacity for delayed gratification, discipline of desires, relational patterns, expectations, and the capacity to cope with conflict or need are all shaped in the family of origin. Much of the strength in ministry is rooted in this solid foundation. However, it is also true that patterns of behaviour, attitudes, and expectations learned in this formative context may prepare us in negative ways. This is not a simple equation. For example, for me, in my family, frugality and duty were high values. Frugality was seen a strength for survival and duty was an obligation. In ministry, both were capable of positive and negative outcomes. Obligation can become oppressive and lead to depression or it may help just get things done. Frugality can inhibit adventuring into new challenges, thus, avoiding risk.

It was under that intense supervision that I had the opportunity to come to understand how I conducted myself in relationships and to see how that was influenced by my family. I learned what it meant to be a middle-child between two brothers and a younger brother to three sisters. Also, I learned what it meant to be a shy person, not overtly competitive, but quite demanding on myself and how to ignore feelings in the interest of duty. It took only four years of the intense pressure of pioneering three churches, the economic limitations of inadequate financial provision, the self-imposed pressure of visitation/evangelism, lack of adequate supervision, and self-doubt to lead me into a very deep depression. I was ready to quit. Much of the pressure was an outcome of growing up in a survival family situation where I learned the value of hard work. But emotional understanding what was not considered very important. Looking back on that experience of over fifty years ago is no longer painful. Help in understanding that my drives had family origins would have been very helpful.

Exploring the input of our families clarifies our responses, values, motivations, and needs. Today, this understanding of self-awareness is often spoken of in terms of mindfulness. In church history, this comes close to the meditative, self-reflective disciplines that were practiced to foster spiritual growth. From a theological perspective, we can look at this from the perspective of God's sovereign involvement in our lives.

One example of this is Jeremiah's call from God.[215] This great prophet resisted by declaring, *"I am only a child."* God message was, *"Before I formed you in the womb, I knew you, before you were born I set you apart; I appointed you as a prophet to the nations."* The Psalmist expressed the same faith. *"I am fearfully and wonderfully made;...My frame was not hidden from Thee when I was made in the secret. When I was skillfully wrought in the depths of the earth. Thine eyes have seen my unformed substance."*[216]

This is a long way from any secular, deterministic view of ourselves. Nor does such thinking give us the illusion of freedom simply to express what we think we want or what expresses ourselves based upon our birth or cultural formation. Indeed, every experience we may define a being negative in our youth may be the shaping of sensitivity, compassion, abilities, and skills that can make us effective in ministry. Many of the most sensitive people in ministry are that way because of a pain that has been redeemed by grace to manifest itself in the ministry to others. Not only the strengths created within us by our families but also the hurts, the pain, and the experiences we found undeserving may be converted into strengths by grace and the transforming of mind and action by the Holy Spirit of God. All the heroes of the faith presented in Hebrews eleven had experienced pain and shortcomings. However, in all of them "whose *weakness was turned to strength*"[217] by their faith in the God, he accomplished his purposes in and through them. We need not hesitate to explore what we bring to ministry from our origins. Our personalities are not locked in place but are open to the transformation God desires for us. In God's economy, what we perceived to be liabilities from our past can, by grace, become assets in our responses in ministry to others. When seen through the prism of faith, liabilities may become assets.

The Educational Experience

How might our education contribute to prevention or open us to intervention? My observations are based on a great deal of experience in education and as an educator in teaching in college, seminary, and university contexts.

Most of these with whom I traveled on their journey in ministry were well educated in theology. It is from this varied perspective that I suggest theological education that is only of an academic nature is inadequate training and preparation for ministry. Please hear me when I say that I speak from within and only to be constructive and helpful.

Education was not a part of my family's experience. I was the only one of six children who had the opportunity of secondary education. My motivation for it was low. Yet in that experience, God touched my life and gave me a motivation to complete the experience. Becoming aware of my great deficiency in Biblical knowledge, I decided to go to seminary for a bachelor's degree in theology to equip me to teach Sunday School. The overpowering passion of my teachers for ministry and especially evangelism, gripped my imagination. I pioneered one church, and then two more after marriage. Evangelism excited me, and God blessed me in bringing many to a new birth in Christ. However, ten semesters of Greek and four in Hebrew, along with great theology and all the instruction received, did not prepare me for raising "babes in Christ" to maturity in their faith. Seven years of this led to the experience of deep depression and frustration in not knowing how to guide people in growth created a crisis.

Most graduates of seminary have very adequate understanding of theology. Few are well educated in human relationships, personal resilience, understanding of ministry issues, or in coping with relationship conflicts. Most have little or no training in the vital area of discipleship or the art of mentoring people to grow in Christ. Some would argue that there needs to be more training in emotional intelligence to compensate intellectual pursuits. These are considered the soft areas in preparation for ministry. An apprenticeship model of education that trains for ministry has advantage over a purely academic model. It is not lack in knowledge of theology but usually lack of knowledge of self, relationships and human relationship issues that trip up people in ministry.

Preparation in Churches

We have not addressed the role that churches should play in setting aside individuals for the ministry. It was the church at Antioch that set aside Paul and Barnabas for ministry.[218] Surely no one would question the role of churches in developing youth in spiritual disciplines, discipleship, and opportunity to discover their gifts which may suit them for ministry. It is in this context, like that of Samuel, where youth could discern the voice of God.[219] The local church could have a powerful role in preparing youth and assisting them in this regard. This may be the best context for youth to grow into a maturity and knowledge that would prepare them for the journey of ministry. Many pastors and missionaries testify to the impact of the pastors or other servants in ministry who have inspired them to seek a seminary education. The personal grounding in knowledge and responsiveness in relationships and sensitivity to the needs of others, if not learned in one's local church, is frequently not learned later. It is in this context that youth could be nurtured in the art of personal care and discipline and the concern for others, which would sustain them in the future challenges of ministry. A local pastor told me he was teaching the teen boys as a means of training his future deacons. In fact, at more than one of those is now preparing for ministry. Compassion for others and personal discipline in spirituality are best learned early in one's life. If is modelled in one's early church life that is a good start.

Imagine how helpful it would be if the art of personal spiritual discipline, learning to hear God's voice, finding God's will, facing the darts of the enemies, wearing the armor of God, learning to delay gratification, developing skills in communication and relationships, and understanding family dynamics were learned in the church's nurture of youth. All these values should be part of the church's curriculum in growing youth to serve Christ. Each church should have a vision for preparing youth for ministry and participating in identifying those gifted of God for the journey of ministry.

The Denomination's Role in Intervention

Based upon my involvement with pastors, I see a great need for denominations to provide both pastors and churches with information, instruction, and guidance for their relationships. For this to happen, there is need for an understanding of the relationship of churches and pastors to the denomination that facilitates interaction and input. It is clear from the New Testament that there was considerable interdependence between churches. Instruction was provided by the Apostolic leadership to elders/pastors and deacons as well as to churches. The instruction of churches involved the respect and honouring of pastors, the care of pastors, and guidance to pastors as to their specific ministry. It would be helpful if denominations provided an articulation of these principles, policies, and processes to both pastors and their churches.

Many pastors, especially those who are experiencing tensions and conflicts, are hesitant to articulate the New Testament-prescribed relationship because it may be interpreted as self-serving. Issues including selection of pastors, provision for pastors, appropriate dealing with community tensions and conflict, and the role of elders and deacons would be more effective if guidelines were provided by the denomination rather than the church's pastor. This can be done from a "service" perspective rather that an "organizational control" perspective. It would be helpful to define the relationship between churches, their pastors, and the denomination to provide some consistency among churches. It is counter-productive to wait until an unresolvable issue arises before the denomination is consulted. It is evident that waiting until a crisis before engaging consultation from outside the church, to provide some objectivity, leads to potential accusation and tension as to whether the denominational leadership is taking the side of the church or the pastor. In my observation, this puts the denomination in an untenable situation.

The clarification and expansion of care for pastors by the denomination may be best expressed in the conferences provided by that denomination's leaders. Many pastors have expressed the desire to avoid conferences that appear to create an opportunity for comparative or competitive interactions on how to simply to do better or to adopt the most recent "successful" fad. Bringing pastors together in a context where vulnerability would be safe, and the needs of pastors addressed, would be of great benefit. This could perhaps be best done at an associational or regional level.

A second opportunity would be to prepare senior or other gifted pastors to become aware of these issues and intervene along the journey of the ministry of their fellow pastors. This would avert the experience of failure in many situations. The practical issues of self-care, identifying tensions early in their development, skills for diffusing conflict, addressing family tensions, and developing emotional intelligence could be part of that.

The issues around leadership are a constant in remedial work with pastors, who have experienced failure. It is common to find that the practices of secular leadership skills when applied to church function create tension in churches. This may be initiated by the pastor in his leadership or elders in their function. In either case it is a major contributor to failure. Much is said about "servant-leadership" which raises many questions about the place of authority in leadership. It is interesting that the concept of servant in the New Testament identifies five different functions of servants or slaves. These ranged over many defined tasks such as, a bonded slave, an attendant, a house-hold servant, a nursing servant and a manager of a household whose chief responsibility was that of stewardship in managing the estate.[220] This requires interpretation as it interacts with the equally important definition of leadership as stewardship. Most of the models of corporate leadership have limited application in the volunteer associations such as churches or the organismic understanding of the Body of Christ. Understanding these issues would forestall much failure. This is too large a topic to address here.

Peer Care and the Spiritual Care Group

One of the most crucial areas in the care of pastors can be provided by another pastor. Ministry is a high-risk occupation.[221] The pastor who seeks to stand alone does not stand long. A study of Paul's experience of ministry clearly indicates the risks.[222] In his writings, he shared his experiences of emotional fatigue, harassment, conflicts from within and without, his thorn in the flesh, and his depth of depression. His salvation was God's coming to him in the person of Titus, his fellow-servant. In his imprisonment in Jerusalem following the confrontation with the council we read, *"The following night the Lord stood near Paul."*[223] Similarly, in the terrible storm at sea he declares, *"Last night an angel of the God to whom I belong and whom I serve stood beside me."*[224] Some seek only the presence of God in their trials. Paul found comfort, refreshment, and nurture among and from his fellow-workers. To isolate one's self in ministry is a sure slide toward failure.

One of the most effective tools for the endurance of pastors is for each to have a Spiritual Care Group wherein continuous support on a consistent basis can be experienced. We need others to stand with us in the role of Jethro in relation to Moses, Paul in relation to his team, or Barnabas as he encouraged others. A spiritual care group is a small group who come together and are committed to provide safety, confidentiality, a listening ear, and a compassionate heart. They meet to support, nurture, comfort, strengthen, and confront each other without judgment. They seek to understand and explore one another's experience while seeking discernment and the guidance of the Holy Spirit in each other's lives. It may involve elements of debriefing, and a reflective pause, to refocus, redefine priorities, recuperate, and enjoy the renewal that comes from being understood. It also helps to find humour in one's experience.

The man of God was never designed to stand alone in ministry. Jethro certainly saw this issue clearly in the life of Moses and intervened.[225] Elijah illustrates the same point, as we have seen earlier. Paul does as well in his depression in Macedonia. Ministry is in community, and the community of one's peers is a safe place to find refuge and support in the stresses of ministry. It is most helpful if this opportunity is planned on a monthly or bi-monthly basis. It is important that there be enough consistency in the frequency of meeting that the anticipation of meaningful sharing is realistic. The context must provide trust, relational integrity, safety, and confidentiality. The ministry of the Spirit of God should be a central focus in this support system. A spiritual care group is essential to endurance in ministry. Therefore, we must guard against such groups descending to a dumping function in complaint.

One may define the role of pastors in relation to each other as that of debriefing each other. I would define debriefing as creating a reflective pause wherein pastors can explore what they are experiencing in ministry without judgement or accusation. Creating a safe and intentionally designed time and place for this kind of helpful interaction has led to great benefit. Debriefing is a form of mentoring at a peer level.

The following is a brief outline that may be useful in planning peer support:

Debriefing Pastors (G. C. Taylor)	
Debriefing is a reflective pause for personal assessment of ministry. The process of debriefing requires:	
• the intentional creation of an opportunity of reflection • on the experience of ministry • with a view to maximizing understanding and learning,	• assessing effectiveness in ministry, and • the impact of one's experience on one's self, spouse, Christian community
Debriefing will involve the following:	
Reflection on • ministry • family • relationships with nationals, missionaries, church, mission	• changes during the term of service and one's response • challenges, successes, stresses, joys • physical well-being and illness
Refocusing through	
• clarifying goals • revising goals	• understanding changing family needs • considering life cycle changes as the may impact ministry
Rearranging priorities	
• in response to growth in ministry skills • in response to changing opportunities of ministry	• in response to changes in organizational priorities
Rest and Recuperation	
• assessing need for rest, recuperation, renewal -spiritual, physical, social, medical • intentionally designing and mapping time for what is needed	• considering training, professional development opportunities or change in ministry

143

> **AN assumption underlying Debriefing is that we have clear goals or objectives against which we measure effectiveness.**

Figure 6.

Additionally, I have found that a guided process of ministry inventory is very helpful. This involves pastors listing every activity in which they are engaged and evaluating each of those activities from several perspectives. I have used a form such as that below. Many have found that through completing this exercise, they clearly define what God has called them to in ministry compared to all the demands that they may experience. If this is shared with church leadership, there can be a partnership in determining priorities, the need for additional staff, or the more careful planning of one's time and function. It helps to clarify what one is gifted and called to do in ministry.

Debriefing Pastors (G. C. Taylor)						
A	B	C	D	E	F	G
Roles	Hours	Gifts	Affirmed	Joy	Valued	Called
1						
2						
Add to as needed						

Column Content:	
A.Role: List all of the roles, functions, tasks, activities and any other ways you use your time in relation to the functions you are expected to fulfill in your current vocational situation.	D.Affirmed: Indicate on a 1-10-point scale the degree to which you are by others affirmed in doing well and effectively the activity indicated.
B. Hours: Indicate the number of hours you would be involved in each "role," etc. during a one-week period. This would be an accumulated number of hours.	E. Joy: Indicate on 1-10-point scale the degree to which you experience joy, fulfillment, pleasure and a sense of accomplishment you experience in this activity.
C.Gifts: Indicate on a 1-10-point scale (10 being high) the degree to which you feel each activity in which you engage uses what you consider to be your gifts and abilities.	F. Valued: Indicate on 1-10-point scale the degree to which you feel the activity represents your value system.
	G.Called: Indicate on 1-10-point scale the degree to which you feel you are fulfilling the call of God on your life in the activity indicated.

Assumptions and Assessment:

The assumption is that if you know your giftedness and acknowledge that giftedness is from God, it follows that God's will would be to engage you in activities that use your giftedness. Also, it is assumed that in fulfilling your giftedness you will experience joy in service and affirmation from others who have spiritual discernment.

Overworked is affirmed in our culture and may be motivated by many variables. Stress will accumulate if we work outside of our giftedness, even if we do so for good reason. This simple exercise may be suggestive of areas in which we should seek adjustment.

Figure 7.

145

Congregational Care of the Pastor

Many pastors who experience failure move toward that destination as a result of failure of the congregation to care for them. That lack of care may be expressed in many ways. Expectations may be overwhelming as many church members have little understanding of the role of the pastor. Also as suggested earlier, pastors are very hesitant to instruct churches for fear of being accused of being self-serving. The greater the gap in understanding between the congregation and the pastor as to that role, the greater the pressure and the likelihood of failure. The failure of elders or deacons to create a system that leads to understanding and accountability is a common contributor. Most frequently, pastors are left to sort things out on their own. Criticism is more common than affirmation.

The Scriptures are abundantly clear. Paul speaks of church leadership as being worthy of *"double honor"* for those engaged in preaching and teaching. He indicates this in relation to financial provision for those *"who direct the affairs of the church."*[226] Great caution is urged in listening to accusations brought against a leader. The writer of Hebrews urges believers to *"remember your leaders"* who were teachers.[227] Paul instructs the church *"to acknowledge those who work hard among you, who care you in the Lord and who admonish you. Hold them in the highest regard in love because of their work."*[228] The word "obey" is often used in the sense of complying with understanding and persuasion rather than what we may call blind obedience or a substitute for each person in their relationship with the Lord, who is the head. It is appropriate in a context of mutual trust and respect within a strong relational component. Paul expected obedience from his friend Philemon.[229] He also expected that people who "risked" (associated with our word gamble) their lives such as Epaphroditus to be honoured for their service.[230] Churches which provide care for their pastors will rarely see a pastor complete the journey toward failure.

Professional Care

It is my contention, after engaging with pastors who experienced failure, that if the dimensions of care suggested above had been provided failure among pastors would be reduced. The would include self-care, appropriate educational training, church involvement in their discipleship and calling, adequate denominational guidance, peer care and congregational care, professional care would have been rarely needed. The time for professional care, whether from medical, psychiatric or psychological intervention, is needed as early as possible in acute situations. Physical health care is essential. A regular check-up should be a requirement for pastors. Unfortunately, many pastors do not disclose enough information to their medical doctors for appropriate decision making. Increased knowledge of symptoms, and a willingness to disclose those early on, is most important in prevention. It is only in a crisis such as trauma, intense conflict, or overwhelming conditions that counselling intervention is needed if the other dimensions of care are sustained in a continuous manner over the career path of ministry.

The following Table provides a simplified summary of the dimensions of care and maintenance for people in ministry. I have used this a check-list to identify short-fall in care. It is useful as a check-list to be sure all the dimensions of care are being provided.

The Care and Maintenance of Pastors (G.C. Taylor)	
I. Divine Care:	**V. Spiritual Care Group:**
• Redemption	• Continuous Support
• Healing	• Accountability
• Holy Spirit Enabling	• Transitional Experience
	• Facing Conflict: Consultation
II. Self Care:	**VI. Denominational Care:**
• Spiritual	• Initiating Ministry
• Emotional	• Crisis Intervention
• Physical	• Transitions in Ministry
• Recreational	• Retirement Preparation
• Social	• Nurturing Development
III. Family Care:	**VII. Church Care:**
• Spousal Relationship	• Honoring the Pastor
• Child Relationships	• Providing for the Shepherd
• Social Relationships	• Nurturing Community support
• Spiritual Engagement	• Environment for Ministry
IV. Peer Care:	**VIII. Professional Care:**
• Friendships	• Medical/Psychiatric/ Psychological
• Mentoring	• Pastoral
• Recreational Associates	• Trauma Response
• Ministry Affirmation	

Figure 8.

The Major Contributors to Pastoral Failure

It is important to be aware of the major contributors that are common to most incidents of pastoral failure. In any of the areas identified earlier, no two journeys were the same. Each person was unique, and each responded to their experience differently. However, the constancy of recurring themes is evident. An attempt to identify these, and their development, will assist in our understanding of how to respond in helpful and redemptive ways.

The Major Spiritual and Emotional Risks of Ministry

Ministry is a glorious calling and an adventure with God. Many who have engaged this vocation would testify to that. We must keep ever before us this reality. It sustains us in the face of the challenges that are inevitable. We see that in the lives of prophets, Apostles, and others in Scripture who served God. Those who have expressed themselves such as Isaiah, Jeremiah, and Paul are explicit in the risks and hardships of ministry but also provide evidence of the fulfillment and joy of knowing God and serving him.

Jesus was very explicit in telling his disciples: "*I have told you these things, so that in me you may have peace. In this world you will have trouble.*"[231] What a contrast! Peace and trouble are experienced simultaneously. He clearly defines their future: "*Then you will be handed over to be persecuted and put to death.*"[232] Jesus did not suggest that the task he was calling the disciples to was going to be an easy one. Remember that he told Peter that he would be sifted as wheat by Satan. Paul was informed that his "*thorn in my flesh*"[233] was a "*messenger of Satan, to torment*" him. There is torment in ministry.

However, it is not only Satan that creates challenges and risks for those in ministry. Paul also speaks of the pressures arising within the churches. These challenges came from members, leaders, and other disrupters.

Further, and more personally, Paul speaks of the "*pressure of my concern*"[234] for those to whom he ministered. The physical, emotional, and spiritual toll he experienced as harassment, which were accentuated by "*fears within*"[235], and the judgment others heaped on him overwhelmed him at times.[236] More than that he recognized that this great treasure, "*the knowledge of the glory of God,*" was resident in "*jars of clay.*"[237] This human vessel experienced being "*hard pressed on every side,*" "*perplexed,*" "*persecuted,*" and "*struck down.*" He declared that death, like the death of Jesus, was at work in him.

149

The pressures of ministry are experienced by each person differently. This must be honoured. There is a correlation between our personalities and what creates pressure or stress for us. Understanding of the dynamic interplay between who one is as a person and what generates anxiety, emotional reactivity or stress as it is experienced by each individual is important to learn. We are susceptible in different ways to Satan's attacks, as well as the impact of others on us, as we interact with people.

All who seek to understand the experience of ministry need to have a realistic picture of what ministry entails. Consider the pressure of Abram in the face of famine for himself and his family, the terror of Elijah who, in a state of exhaustion, was threatened with immediate death and then physically abused himself in great physical exhaustion, or Peter, feeling abandoned by the one he believed to be the Messiah and challenged by those who were abusing the one he thought to be the Christ. Then, we must seek to understand the journeys of Jim, Mel, and Jordon as they faced spiritual and emotional turmoil.

Failure cannot be understood without grasping the risks—spiritually and emotionally—of engaging in ministry. Jordon's experience was heightened by the fact that he was driven by intrinsic pressures to serve others. Those motivated by extrinsic values respond to demands differently. When driven from within, it is often the case that one is being driven by one's own needs. That subjectivity destroys objectivity and the ability to let go when not engaged.

Disenchantment with Leadership

Consider with me the challenges of leadership in ministry. Walk with Moses, the reluctant leader, who faced the grumbling, accusations, anger, and disloyalty from those God called him to lead. Consider David who had been chosen and anointed by Samuel to be the future King. He faced the animosity of King Saul in his emotionally distraught state of depression. He faced hunger and deprivation hiding in the wilderness and was rejected and hounded. In our day, we define battle fatigue as PTSD and certainly after the years of war, David would have qualified; as would Elijah and Peter.

In the stories of the pastors, we see Jim disillusioned by the deception that characterized his elders in their leadership. Similarly, with Mel, as he was pressured to accomplish more. Then, with good intention put poor planning, he was pushed into defeat as he was required to manage a large team chosen by others. Jordon was abandoned by his lead pastor and his work undermined by those who controlled the purse strings in his church. These individuals where not only disenchanted by the leaders they worked with but by the expectations laid on them for their role in leadership.

The culture expectations of leadership are often presented as a choice between following a corporate, management, military, coaching, or political model. None of these models fit the model of the church as a community of believers who are gifted by God with roles consistent with those gifts but functioning in the unity of an organism designed to manifest the "life of Jesus" in our lives as a community.

If I may venture to suggest, biblical leadership is all about relational functioning and may be from within, from behind, from in front, from above, or from outside. I call this positional leadership. It requires flexibility to move into different dimensions of leadership that is required by each situation. Leadership is not static but dynamic and responsive to the context. As members of an organism, the body, we are to function in a coordinated and complimentary manner that recognizes the contribution of each member. Christ is the head, the authority.[238] What is referred to as the servant model of leadership must take into consideration that in the slave culture of the New Testament there were at least five levels of functioning among slaves.[239] To understand the servant model of leadership, one must define the level relationally in which the slave was functioning. Stewardship is an effective definition of leadership. This implies the management of resources.

The pastors with whom I've counselled, who had journeyed to failure, all exhibited a poor understanding of leadership. Many were deeply unhappy and negatively impacted by secular leadership practices of elders and other leaders in the churches they served. Many were deeply frustrated by the lack of leadership in ministry of people within the congregation. Often, the style of leadership of pastors is quite inflexible, lacks integrity, or functions in a control mode. Or they saw their role as a servant (slave) to the interests of others. As in the case of Jordon, he was consumed by his need to respond to the needs of all; essentially to meet his needs and hoping that in doing so he would meet the needs of others. Mel obviously resisted the role of supervising, nurturing, or managing the ministry of others.

Those pastors who seemed most effective in leadership functioned from a position of trust and influence. Seeing leadership as a gift that others give you and as an act of stewardship was rarely evident. Leadership may best be defined as stewardship of the resources God has placed in the persons for whom one is responsible as a pastor. Leadership issues play a big role in leading people on the journey toward failure. Frequently, leadership issues lead to extreme loneliness as may be seen in the experience of Mel, Jim and Jordon.

Conflicts of Priority: Ministry or Family

If a pastor is married, invariably the issue of the priority of ministry and family becomes an issue. In our stories, Abraham and Sarah illustrate some of these concerns. Also, the tensions created in the family of Jim and Mel became acute. The issue of inadequate financial resources contributed to Jim and Sally's loss of relationship. The frugality learned in his family of origin was a handicap in Jim's case as he felt it was his lot to endure. The necessity of his wife working contributed to the loss of relationship and of the support Jim needed from Sally. Home schooling places strain on the spousal relationship and, in some cases, parents are not able to bridge the difference between being a parent and a teacher. The pressure for Mel arose from conflicting expectations of his children and his absorption in ministry which added to the children's frustration. This tension angered his wife who had to deal with the outcomes of that tension as it manifested itself in the home.

A common denominator in family issues is the degree to which the couples seek, experience, and determine how to fulfil the call of God together. The pressure for wives to have a professional, self-fulfilling career has increased greatly in our culture. Additionally, children in our culture are sometimes defined as a liability which interferes with the lifestyle that parents desire. In our Canadian culture, government-controlled institutions such as schools and day care are assuming the parental role. Parents have less and less control over the curriculum.

The "glass-house" experience is an element in the minds of some pastors, spouses and children as they experience expectations from church members. Rebellious children, as in the case of Eli[240], may become an issue. Excessive demands on "pastor's kids" create great problems in the family and often in their later lives. It is painful to hear a pastor raise the question of whether he should leave the ministry because his children have turned against the church or the Lord. It is my observation that in many cases, the rebellion of children can be traced back to church experience. If the pastor has experienced church conflict, it will often negatively impact the children. For example, if children are younger when conflict occurs, the child will often harbour that unconsciously in their mind until they reach the teen years and, then, will begin to act out by withdrawing from the church. Sometimes, this is expressed in rebellion.

Sometimes, a young person will experience friendship, acceptance, and community in a secular university of a quality they did not experience in church. This may be coupled with the development of critical skills and encouragement to be their own person and escaping the controls of home. Encouraged by peers, they may withdraw from spiritual activity or reject the faith of their parents. This has happened often enough to constitute a pattern I have witnessed in my experience with families of pastors. If these youth witnessed conflict in the church where they thought dad was being abused, they are ripe for rejecting church and/or Christianity. It is sad to witness these behaviours, especially if what they have interpreted from limited and youth perspectives may not represent what really happened.

When ministry becomes the mistress, spouses feel abandoned. Of course, children are very sensitive to the loss of father when dad is consumed by activity or overwhelmed by the pressure of ministry. This creeping vine of over-engagement or anxiety-induced preoccupation cunningly chokes the joy of life out a family in its consumption of the pastor's time. The insidious growth slowly, sometimes imperceptibly, consumes time, energy, and emotional reserve and it generates anxiety. It robs the pastor of the necessary spousal support that often enables endurance in ministry.

It is critical that ministry be defined as the ministry of the family rather than simply the ministry of the pastor. These considerations are best sorted out at the beginning of courtship rather than after marriage. Unity within the spousal relationship is foundational. If one is single when called, it is crucial to sort out the ministry expectation with a potential spouse and to be sure that God's call is to the couple as a unity. The individualism practised today where in each spouse must experience personal fulfillment unrelated to their unity in marriage is untenable. The stresses of ministry require unity of commitment. Engagement of children in the experience of ministry while protecting them from what they do not have the capacity to understand is equally important. Having walked through these issues with scores of missionary kids indicates the problem as being acute in that community also.

Finding a balance in dedication to ministry and dedication to family is a necessity for those engaged in ministry when married. The pastoral role cannot be defined as that of a monk or hermit. If the choice to marry is in God's will and ministry is a response to his call, a balance is necessary to fulfill his will. To fail in finding that balance is to fail in one's service to God as well as to fail in one's responsibilities to spouse and children. A double failure is the outcome. In reality, it is a mixed life. Neither component can be jettisoned in the interest of the other. The expectations of others may create tensions but our responsibility before God is clear.

Retreat into Loneliness, Depression and Despair

The progression of this trio of emotions is evident in Elijah, Jim, Mel, and Jordon. The spiral begins innocently enough. Self-question, without resolution or objectivity, leads to self-doubt and circular reasoning continues the descent. When one becomes imprisoned in the dark dungeon of rumination, there is little hope of breaking out alone. If one looks at the comparative chart provided earlier, it is very evident that the downward emotional journey is quite predictable and consistent. The physical exhaustion becomes paired with emotional weariness. Chronic stress leads to chronic fatigue. These, in turn, issue in frustration, blaming of others, the internalization of anger, and self-accusation. When one does not have the freedom to explode in anger, whether because of fear of reprisal or the negation of anger, it is normal to implode. People who do not acknowledge and vent their anger will usually internalize it into self-blame. This turning on one's self is typical for those who do not understand that anger is most frequently a response to a breach of values, expectations and self-worth.[241] Anxiety turned inward escalates with the ambiguity of self-knowledge and clouded by the confusion of the moment. Perhaps there is no better description of this than that provide by the Psalmist. "When I kept silent, my bones wasted away through my groaning all day long." (Psalm 32:3) Depression is a cruel master and breaks the heart and mind that hosts it. The cruelty of judgment is most harsh when it is directed toward one's self. When we turn upon ourselves in depression, it is akin to cannibalism. The soul consumes itself in despair when a sense of loneliness is captured and nurtured. As it is nurtured it grows to maturity in cynicism.

The sense of being betrayed, as illustrated by Jordon, more overtly further pushes one into one's self. There are many related variables in personality that determine one's pattern. Anger is a built-in neurological and chemical response of the body to threat. However, there is much in anger that is an expression of learned behaviour. Lack of understanding of this, coupled with a lack of freedom or context to safely explore these feelings, lead to internalization. Jordon illustrated this conundrum. He cared out of compulsive need to do so driven from within. His isolation of himself in responding to need left no time for his unacknowledged needs to be himself. He was ripe for catastrophe. It is like the person who takes poison, hoping that the enemy will die. An analogy might help.

In North America, a vine introduced in the 1800's is now becoming a problem. It is called the Dog-strangling vine, which grows rapidly in almost any circumstance. It wraps itself around other plants, trees, fences, or anything in its reach. It has peculiar pods which snap open, at the right time, with great force, throwing its seeds far and wide. As it wraps its tentacles around anything, it begins to strangle it. It creates matted colonies in which only it can survive. It is toxic to animals and insects. It squeezes life out of what it touches.

In the same way the emotional despair that develops in pastors on the road to failure, renders them lifeless—lethargic in mind, spirit and body. Strangulation by emotional despair is a sure killer. The Old Testament writer, Job, would identify with pastors in this state. In his despair he said, "*I am seething within, and cannot relax.*" It becomes a spiritual problem as he declares, "*He (God) has loosed His bowstring and afflicted me.*"[242] Social isolation and abandonment by God become confused. The deep darkness is like the blackness we experience when all the lights go out. There is no direction and no hope in finding one's way. The thoughts become a whirlpool of emotion and reason confused by shame when one is gripped by self-condemnation.

A tragic accompaniment to this process is the retreat into isolation and loneliness. This was the experience of Elijah, perhaps David, and certainly, Jim, Mel, and Jordon. Starving for nurture and sustenance, they turned inward until they found comfort in illicit and inappropriate ways. When Jim wrapped himself in his own brokenness, it echoed with the brokenness in his elders' board; creating a cacophony of deafening sound. His own brokenness multiplied his despair of ever entering the brokenness of others.

The despair of loneliness is unendurable for long. If it does not lead to immorality, it frequently leads to suicide or severe emotional problems. Humans were not designed for loneliness. When loneliness is sought in response to immorality it leads to secrecy. Secrecy robs one of speech the vehicle for being known which comes through communion with others. The loss of a sense of community is evident in the pastors' experience. They retreated into themselves. We are never enough for ourselves. Self-fulfillment is an illusion as we cannot be fulfilled without the engagement of others in our lives. Many have captured the experience of loneliness. T.S. Elliot wrote:

"…..Hell is oneself,
Hell is alone, the other figures in it
Merely projections. There is nothing to escape from
And nothing to escape to. One is always alone."[243]

Silence accompanies loneliness. Each of the four (Elijah, Jim, Mel, and Jordon) illustrated that they substituted self-talk for communication with others. Self-talk short-circuits the relationality we were created for. The loss of nurturing communication with elders, fellow-workers, and spouses was profound. This is very much the case with pastors who are extroverts. Silence not only robs one's self of hearing one's thoughts expressed out loud, but it also robs the spouse of engagement and understanding. It shocked me when I asked a priest what he thought about a topic of common interest and he replied, "I don't know, I haven't said it yet." He was stating a profound truth. We often don't know what we think about something until we have had the opportunity to share it with others and, in the process, clarify our own thinking. Obviously, in doing so we may benefit from the response and additional insight of another.

But silence is also cruel in what it does to others. It leaves them to guess what we are thinking. That is a most dangerous game. The likelihood of another guessing what our silence means is probably nil. Thus, we are damaged by silence and we damage others who are important to us. Love is lost when there is no listening ear to hear one's pain. When this stage of the journey toward failure is reached, we are near the destination of failure. That failure is often expressed in sin. Silence is an expression of fear as Matthew Arnold captured it.

> "I knew the mass of men concealed
> Their thoughts, for fear that if revealed
> They would by other men be met
> With blank indifference, or with blame reproved..."[244]

Loneliness is one of the nails that fasten the coffin on pastoral ministry. Glowing coals, separated from the nurture and heat of like substance, cools to ash. Starved for objective and stimulating conversation, reflection and feedback, one dries up and chokes on the dust of loneliness.

Jordon illustrates another dynamic that happens often. The people, to whom he ministered, loved his care. But they sometimes confused their love of his compassion with love for him. His very desperate need for self-care and care from others became confused when he mistook his client's love of his care for love for him personally. He needed the objectivity of seeing himself as a vehicle of God's love and grace. This would enable him to differentiate between their love of his service and their appreciation him as the mediator of that grace. This is a common trap into which people-helpers are prone to fall. The intimacy of ministry provides a risky context for pastors who have great personal needs or under the pressure of ministry. The applauding of pastoral compassion may also contribute to its excesses.

Pressure from Stage of Life Issues

Ministry experience and issues change as one travels the career path of ministry. Early in ministry one is seeking to define priorities, develop a style of ministry, clarification of expectations of others and of self, the balance of ministry with other life demands, and a multitude of other concerns. Of course, learning the art of sermon preparation occupies energy.

After ten to fifteen years in ministry, the challenges change. One may be in a comfortable groove. Or, one may be experiencing the pressure of a successful church growth resulting in increased pressure. In my ministry to pastors, I have found many stressed by these increased demands. They question whether they can maintain the pace and the multiplicity of tasks that larger responsibility brings. If additional staff is added, the issue of management becomes acute. Mel illustrated these issues. Popularity or effective ministry may lead to expectations or desires for broader ministry.

The mid-years bring different demands. Often in the forty-five to fifty-five range, pastors are wondering if this is all there is. Physical limitations may begin to appear. The children's educational needs are becoming acute. The question of "how much longer?" or, "what do I do in retirement?" emerge. Some pastors have experienced church growth that requires new building expansion. They ask themselves, "Am I prepared to commit to long-term to see that through?" If illness has become a part of the family equation, that can be stressful. Issues of contentment rise to the surface. As children grow older, marry, and bear grandchildren, the tug of wishing to spend more time with them or to be closer to them becomes an issue. Then the larger issue of retirement becomes acute. Where to live? When to retire? What to do in retirement? Are resources adequate? The stress related to stages of life, if coupled with the problems listed above create large issues for pastors.

All the five experiences we have mentioned required intervention. Issues are best discussed and thought through before they become acute. When they begin to take on a life of their own, it is more difficult to understand or cope with. They develop subtly, without invitation. They have dramatic effect of the well-being of a pastor in every dimension of his life. They are the contributing factors that continually push pastors along the journey toward failure. If dealt with when they are beginning or small, they can be readily managed. However, once they grow, they become like the strangling vine which destroys whatever it clings to. They suck the life out pastors and propel them toward that undesirable destination of failure.

Summary:

1. There are many examples of Biblical interventions.
2. People often respond negatively to accusation but more helpfully to exploration.
3. Prevention is often much more effective if it is defined as early intervention in the journey of ministry.
4. There are many approaches to care along the career path of ministry that are effective in prevention.
5. There are several early experiences that are indicators of movement toward failure.

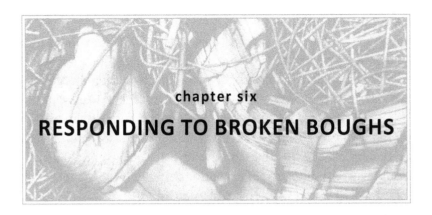

chapter six

RESPONDING TO BROKEN BOUGHS

IN THIS CHAPTER, WE LOOK AT ALTERNATIVE RESPONSES TO THE servants of God who become broken boughs in ministry. It will be clear that early intervention is the best response. A realistic understanding of ministry along with a support system that engages self, family, denomination, church, and peers will go a long way in forestalling failure.

Not Responding as the World

However, failure in ministry is a reality, even if prevention and intervention have been initiated through nurturing support. We must address the consideration of a response to those incidents. A plan of redemptive response, based not only on accountability, truth, and justice but also consistent with the Christian faith, is needed.

We must slow the response process down so that a prayerfully determined one that honours everyone involved is followed. Reactive responses generate results that are unproductive and chase people into retreat. At that point, truth and confusion become mixed in a concoction of anxiety and denial. Denial is usually a response to accusation, intimidation, fear, and the absence of grace or understanding. This discussion will seek to be concise in suggesting some of the key elements in the process of responding to sin in the life of a pastor.

Responding to Accusations

Sometimes suspicion, hearsay, or second-hand information raises questions of the pastor's conduct. Other times the body language or a mood change in the pastor can indicate a deep struggle is present. When evidence appears, it must be taken seriously.

The leadership person who has the most trusting relationship should be the one to approach the pastor. This must be done with gentleness, sensitivity, and tentativeness. If this is a possibility, I would consider it a pre-confrontational stage. It is best to make the approach in the safety of trust and confidentiality. Care must be taken because of its limitation in this context. We must make a commitment to confidentiality for a limited time until an understanding is achieved or until the spouse or family have been informed or engaged. It will essentially take the form of a request to explore what the pastor is dealing with. Presented in the right way, it will lead to openness rather than defensiveness.

Unfortunately, in many situations, the process begins with an accusation, which frequently is responded to with defence. A gentler approach is more likely to be successful and to lead to an acknowledgment of the pastor's struggle and an openness to further discussion. This must not be staged as an adversarial relationship resembling a court room. A better analogy is Paul's encouragement in Galatians 6:1-5. Here the intent is restoration and the approach is to be with gentleness.

Frequently, this type of approach will lead to an invitation to meet specifically to discuss where things are at from the pastor's perspective. This will often lead to an acknowledgement of issues and, if it is present, the acknowledgement of sin. I cannot emphasize too strongly the advantage of creating an environment of openness that encourages free confession rather than a forced confession under the duress of threat. It needs to be clearly understood that confession at this point is very likely of a limited value, but it is a better place to start. Gentle listening is much more likely to lead to confession than is confrontation or accusation. The hope of being understood will contribute to an effective understanding of the situation. Matthew 18[245] clearly indicates that confrontation must be approached as a process. These principles should be considered in connection with Paul's exhortation to bear one another's burdens and the focus of James on prayer and confession.[246]

If there is no openness to the invitation to explore the concerns, then, one moves to a more formal meeting in which the evidence at hand is shared explicitly but also with care and gentleness. Remember Paul's urgent suggestion, *"Do not entertain an accusation against an elder unless it is brought by two or three witnesses."*[247]

It is far more effective to invite disclosure than it is to bring accusation that leads to a defensive response. The careful assessment of the validity and personal integrity of the source of information must be substantiated. I have been involved in situations where accusations were received and acted on, which then led to great damage. Then later, a discovery revealed the accusations to be of a malicious nature. If children are involved care must be taken to appropriately engage parents and to adequately assess the child's understanding and level of comprehension. Great care must be taken in determining a process that is consistent with our Christian convictions as well as the need to fulfill our legal obligations.

One of the significant issues is that the persons in spiritual leadership may not be equipped to deal with an issue of moral failure. They were elected to provide spiritual care and leadership to the congregation. I have counselled with elders who became very damaged by the process of having to deal with pastoral failure. They, too, need care and guidance in order to cope with the process. Paul provides some suggestion concerning the selection of individuals to arbitrate in church issues. It is evident that these were not always people in leadership. There may be other criteria that are important. (1 Corinthians 6)

Many denominations have outlined processes to deal with accusations. I would urge churches to access that wisdom. If a preliminary confession is made, it is then appropriate to discuss the most beneficial way forward. Here again, it is best to approach this as a problem to be solved rather than a judgment to be handed down from a place of authority.

It is helpful at this point to understand the difference between judgment and discernment. These are closely related words in Scripture, but they are words with significant distinction. The word "to judge" is quite strictly reserved for a forensic setting wherein an authoritative person representing the state is pronouncing guilt and sentencing from his dais of power. Judgment generates reaction and rarely leads to an acceptance of responsibility for sin. Discernment is a process of laying things out in clarity so that the differences are visible, and choices made between the alternatives. It is much more a pursuit of understanding that will inform the decision. When decisions are made based on evidence which is not explored to achieve understanding, a defensiveness is raised in order to find flaws in the evidence and to create doubt.

Many times, this is the experience of accused pastors. The powerful example of Nathan in confronting David has much to teach us. Nathan told a story which clarified, and bought to the fore of his thinking, the values that were of great importance to David. Only when the values and morality of the situation was clear did Nathan confront David with the words, "You are the man." The confrontation of pastors would be more effective if the engagement of confrontation was of a similar mode. To begin with the clarification of values and commitments that may have been preached may achieve several things. It may get people on the same page. It may also define the issue more clearly. It enables one to come alongside the person and define the issue between him and his values or him and God rather than focusing of the offence to the church.

The prime issue is not the way the pastor has breached the values of the leadership of the church, nor even the offence to the church. The primary issue is the pastor's breach of his own values and the values that he has committed himself to as a follower of God. If the nature of the confrontation is between the pastor and his own values—and between him and God, then those doing the confrontation can be there to respond to the pastor's needs in a non-judgemental manner. Thus, even the word "accusation" may not be best at this stage.

A redemptive approach does not set aside truth or consequences but clarifies the reality that sin is first against God and self. David knew this, *"Against Thee, Thee only, I have sinned, and done what is evil in Thy sight."*[248] David was very aware that his sin impacted many and had severe consequences, which continued through his entire life. To approach the situation first as a personal affront or a breach of contract with the church or its leadership may lead to an adversarial response. Seeking to understand from the perspective of the offender is much more an approach of grace. It is more a case of coming along side of the person to respond to the needs of all impacted. Looking at the issue from a broader perspective than just the guilt of the pastor is much more likely to bring clarity and elicit openness. Bringing the issues into focus in a context of seeking God's way forward requires the pursuit of truth, rather than accusation, until the facts are fully understood. Putting it simply, full understanding should be sought rather than leaping to the issues of guilt and judgment. This may take some time, but it will be well spent.

James provided some very astute advice in his epistle. He discussed the confession of sins to each other. His first encouragement was to pray and to seek to live together "whole and healed." He concluded, *"My dear friends, if you know people who have wandered off from God's truth, don't write them off. Go after them. Get them back and you will have rescued precious lives from destruction and prevented an epidemic of wandering away from God.'*[249]

Discerning a Plan Forward

Discipline is an expression of love. If we think long-term, we must begin the process of dealing with moral failure from a redemptive, rather than punitive, perspective. This does not in any way mitigate guilt or responsibility. Nor does it set aside appropriate disciplinary action. However, it will greatly influence the process and the outcome. It is essential that those who first deal with a pastor who has failed, do so with grace and firmness. The more understanding and grace shown toward the pastor at this point the more readily will he respond to the work of the Spirit of God in what follows. The decision to terminate the services of the pastor, either temporarily until further understanding is achieved or permanently, is a crucial one. Clarity which avoids ambiguity and confusion is what we must strive for. Each needs clarity of expectations, both elders and pastor.

In the case of temporary termination, a time period of a few months is best. Then at that point, there can be a reassessment of the situation and the pastor's progress towards reconciliation. If resignation is indicated, severance considerations become important. Concern for the family's needs, the emotional state of those involved, and the possibility of employment need to be fairly addressed. Length of service prior to the incident will influence the financial considerations. As a general rule, generosity in severance arrangements concerning finances and communication with the congregation will encourage peaceful separation and gratitude. It will also encourage more wholesome and helpful attitudes in both the congregation and the pastor and his family. Financial generosity is a small price to pay if it encourages a redemptive opportunity. Many pastors do not have large financial reserves and family provision becomes a major concern. Many churches have included as part of the severance package adequate funds to facilitate professional help, if that is needed. Protection of the family from any punitive expressions or any unwise defence of the pastor from the congregation is necessary.

The general principle seems to be that the greater the generosity of the church, the more likely the pastor and family will be to seek help. Frugality at this point generally produces anger and a reaction that is counterproductive. The needs and redemption of all concerned is a greater consideration than any punitive intent or financial costs.

Expectations concerning the pastor's ongoing contact with the congregation need to be addressed. Pushing the pastor and his family into further isolation is usually detrimental. However, permitting access to the congregation usually leads to further division. An alternative is to set up a small mediating committee which can work with the pastor to avoid total disconnect, and to assist those in the congregation who need help coping with the pastor's fall. It is often helpful to have a small group chosen by giftedness to focus on the care of the congregation. They do not focus on the pastor's experience but the need of those in the congregation who need ministry. Often, those involved in dealing with the pastor are not the best ones for this role. Secondly, it is most necessary to provide a Spiritual Care Group (often best from among pastoral peers) to focus on the spiritual recovery of the pastor. In most cases the best route to follow is to employ a wise, intentional interim pastor with a high level of relational skill and the ability to be firm but sensitive in hearing the concerns of people. There needs to be a mediator between the church leadership, who are dealing with the pastor, and the congregation.

A major problem is that the congregation will be divided. The level of trust between the leadership and the congregation will be tested. There will be those who in sympathy for the pastor who will judge any action as to severe. Others will want maximum retaliation, often as an expression of hurt, legalism, or an attempt to vindicate God's punishment of sin. Bridging these differences is a major issue for church leadership. Often, bringing in an objective perspective is helpful. That may mean soliciting denominational leadership, an intentional interim pastor, or professional guidance—or all three. Openly acknowledging the differing perspectives in the congregation and dealing with the emotions of guilt, sorrow, grief, hurt, and disillusionment is necessary. The healing of the congregation is a crucial responsibility of the leadership. Confusion among congregational members, such as rumours or misinformation, if permitted to circulate unabated, is very destructive. It can be curtailed by a careful provision of information that assures that those engaged are doing their job with due diligence and care. It is important to assure the congregation that all of the people impacted are being appropriately ministered to as wisely as possible.

Summary of Principles
1. Slow the process to achieve full understanding before decision-making
2. Manifest grace and gentleness
3. Access denominational guidelines
4. Seek discernment rather than judgment
5. Create a context conducive to confession rather than accusation
6. Think redemptively rather than punitively
7. Be cautious with information received from accusations
8. Clarify values that have been breached in the experience
9. Address congregational needs and differences
10. Acknowledge the limitations of immediate repentance and confession

Figure 9.

Confession and Repentance

Usually, church leadership, when dealing with pastoral failure, anticipate confession and repentance. This is usually a disappointment. Ready confession normally indicates an acknowledgement of being caught. Such acknowledgement should be simply defined as such and not labelled as a confession. There is a great gulf between admission and confession. Because of the pervasive effect of sin, it is best to wait until all the repercussions of one's behaviour have been identified before one confesses.

Most pastors, in my experience, are not able to confess until they have had opportunity to explore the total ramifications and impact of their actions. This will not be complete until the Spirit of God has worked the work of conviction with respect to the magnitude of the sin and its consequences. Pastors I have counselled are far more aware of what is to be confessed after much deeper of exploration over extended time into what led up to the behaviour and its consequences. To rush confession is to minimize its meaning.

There is much that can be done to encourage confession. The offer of acceptance and love in the face of sin will facilitate confession much more than any harsh, legalistic reaction to sin. The wisdom of Nathan, as noted earlier, was that he led David to a clarification of his values and commitments before he confronted him. Nathan came alongside of David as a friend and mentor as well as a messenger of God. David had hidden his sin for a significant time. He clutched his sin to his chest and rested in the disquiet of his silence.

One of the major factors in confession is the breaking of the silence. People who hide their sin become hardened in that hiddenness. Confession is taking the covers off and exposing one's self to others. The magnitude of this step needs to be understood. Pornography among pastors is a hidden activity. Moral failure is of such magnitude that one develops skills in hiding it from all, often even from one's self through denial or rationalization to avoid self-confrontation. Confession means disclosure, vulnerability, becoming naked before people who have looked up to them, and facing the horror of their condemnation. If we can appreciate the magnitude of what the pastor is being called to do in confession, one may be able to be gentle but forthright in this process. The depth of shame, though unexpressed, is often very overwhelming. That, couple with the profound sense of failure difficult to cope with quickly.

We need to remember that sin can never staunch the love of God, if we confess in repentance. It is love in the face of sin that generates confession and repentance. Paul declared, *"God's kindness is intended to lead you to repentance."*[250] God's kindness is manifest in *"the incomparable riches of his grace, expressed in his kindness."*[251] The word "kindness" is sometime translated goodness.

Paul also sees a relationship between "godly sorrow" and repentance. The sorrow the Corinthians experience was the result of being confronted by Paul. The mutual respect, concern, and affection between Paul and the Corinthian believers were an important part of this dynamic.

Scripture clearly states that repentance is the work of the Holy Spirit and is evidenced by sorrow and grief. Repentance is, first, an acknowledgement of sin against God but it also clearly sees the consequences of the ripple effect of one's sin on the ever-widening circles of others.[252]

Sin that occurs in the theatre of the imagination is often more difficult to deal with when it comes to confession and repentance. Sometimes repentance and confession are made difficult because of the inadequacy of our internal critic, which leads to the kind of conflict Paul described.[253] Sin is like a prison: "*Bring my soul out of prison*," cried the Psalmist.[254] Having worked for some years in a prison setting, I understand to some extent the fear of the person being set free from prison. It may seem strange, but many pastors fear the freedom that confession and repentance brings because of the comfort of the dreaded but safe silence in which they have dwelt. Coming into the brightness of full confession and repentance can be very frightening. Moving from the darkness of despair and loneliness in secret guilt into the bright light of truth and openness is a large step that feels frightening. Understanding the magnitude of this movement may help in increasing our sensitivity. We need to take people by the hand offering assistance when encouraging that step.

My experience would suggest that confession and repentance at the time of confrontation is rarely adequate. Therefore, as important as it is, it is only a first step. It usually requires much deeper exploration to discover the full extent of confession and repentance. After months of a guided exploration into the journey to failure, pastors are much more adequately equipped to fully confess and repent. If too much is made of the initial confession, it may greatly inhibit the full exploration of the sin in its insidious entrapping. A study of the confessional psalms of David helps greatly in understanding this principle. Those Psalms were the result of much exploration into the depths of his sinfulness. Pastors need time to explore the reasons for their sin before full confession and repentance can be expected.

Responding to Confessed Sin

Let me summarize by acknowledging that pastors caught in the trap of failure and sin, for whatever reason, respond very differently. Very few respond with the arrogance of willful disobedience such as Jonah demonstrated. His choice to run away from God's command was a willfully planned rebellion. Most frequently, pastors, who end up at the terminal point of brokenness in ministry, do not fully understand how this happened in their lives. They find themselves in a "dark night of the soul" and wonder how they arrived there. In most cases, the straw that broke the camel's back was something they fell into while in despair. In many cases it is not clear whether they were victims of a predator or if, in a time of weakness, they succumbed to emotions they did not have the strength to resist. Most have arrived at a very dark place before the fatal choice was made. Yes, it often is a choice, but it is an action taken under great duress and emotional confusion.

The church leadership that confronts the accusation must understand this experience from the perspective of the pastor. This will vary depending on many factors. Often it is like coming out of a very dark, dingy cave into the brilliant sunlight. Moving from the black darkness of silence and secrecy into the luminous light of facing the truth of brokenness is a frightful experience. The question of how people will respond and who will be impacted is a great burden to take up. The road from despair and loneliness, self-condemnation, and guilt to the freedom of confession and repentance is not an easy road. Those dealing with a pastor who is broken bough must understand the trauma of confession and repentance and the implications which are nightmarish to the pastor.

Acknowledging the pain for the pastor does not set aside the consequences. However, it certainly creates a better understanding and provides a map of grace and gentleness in confronting the situation. Confrontation must be accompanied by both an acceptance of a fellow-sinner and the hope of the grace of God, administered by the Holy Spirit. True conviction is a gift of the Spirit of God; but is often hampered by the attempt of others to convict in judgment.

The offer of assistance in moving forward does not set aside the necessity for clarifying the need of confession and repentance to whatever extent a pastor is able to express it. The pastor needs to be assured that he will be dealt with graciously and respectfully, and that his family will be also ministered to in acceptable and helpful ways. Providing time for the pastor to disclose to his spouse and family is crucial. Someone may go with him to support him in that process.

Any communication with the church needs to be carefully planned. It is important not to overstate or understate the issues at this point. The congregation will need assurance that the issues are being addressed and that when all the facts and implications are worked out, they will be communicated.

Limitations on the pastor and the congregation regarding communication, contact, explanation, or any other information, require clarification and restriction. The pastor is not the best one, at this point, to talk to the congregation. It is usually premature for a pastor to express confession or repentance immediately. More complete understanding is needed. Considerations of severance are crucial as was discussed earlier.

When Others Are Impacted
If there was immoral involvement with another, it becomes important to respond to the needs of that person also. However, it is important not to assume total innocence of any participating individuals until that is clearly established. The openness of the other person to receive ministry becomes a key issue. This must

be explored carefully without assumptions. Mutual responsibility is most frequently achieved when all the facts are known. In some cases, it has become clear to me that the pastor was as much a victim as a perpetrator. One must be cautious in moving to quickly to conclusions.

It is usually necessary at this point to engage denominational guidance and professional help. It is desirable to furnish funds to provide professional counselling for the pastor, the family and any other participants as part of the severance package. Clarity as to expectations as to the amount these funds and the acknowledgement of the confidentiality of professional counselling is important to establish. Expectations concerning any reporting of the counsellor to the church leadership requires clarification at the beginning. Much confusion in the future is avoided if clarity of expectations is understood.

The role of the denomination also needs clarification. Their role is primarily an administrative function focusing on protecting the denomination and assuring issues related to credentialing are appropriately cared for. My experience suggests the redemptive relationship is the responsibility of the church, its leadership and membership.

Churches are different than Corporations

It is important that church leadership understand that dismissal within a church context is very different than in a secular context. The contract between an employer and employee in the secular context is based upon salary in exchange for productive involvement toward the goals of the organization. A breach in that contract may be settled in financial and legal terms.

The situation is very different in a church. The church is the body of Christ and as such is like a family of interdependent and closely related individuals. The view of the church as a body with different members providing different functions is important. The severance of an arm is not a small matter. It affects the entire body. The relationship of brothers to each other changes the dynamic.

One is not dealing with an employee but a fellow-believer for whom we have responsibility. Our primary responsibility to one of our members who sins is to restore that one.[255] Whatever action is taken must be done in keeping with these principles.

Restoration to Fellowship and/or Ministry

The questions concerning restoration to fellowship and reinstatement in ministry are often confused. When they are mixed together, it invariably leads to further confusion. Restoration to fellowship with believers and restoration to fellowship with the church to which the pastor was leading are two different actions. First, care needs to be taken in encouraging the pastor and his family to find a place of fellowship where they can find acceptance and ministry. It is usually not adequate to simply leave this responsibility to the pastor. The community of faith is larger than the church to which the pastor belonged. Although there are exceptions, there are good reasons for the family not continuing in the church where he pastored when the offence was committed. This places pressure on both the pastor and his family to share with the congregation. However, there are illustrations where pastors have experience healing in the same church in which they had served. The tensions created by the differing responses of the congregation often leads to much confusion. It is helpful if it is explained to the church that the pastor and his family will be attending elsewhere. Often helpful guidance about continuing contact with the pastor needs to be clarified as to the degree to which that is appropriate. Some members will want to express themselves in grief, appreciation, and care. Others will want to express judgment and disappointment. Acknowledging the different responses is appropriate. Often, it is best to encourage written or electronic communication rather than personal contact. It is a tightrope between abandoning and caring for the pastor and his family.

The Biblical emphasis on restoration is a mandate that should not be ignored. It may take months or, in some cases, years to accomplish. However, at some point, it is usually very helpful to have a service of restoration to fellowship. If this is coupled with an opportunity for the pastor to more adequately clarify and articulate his journey both to failure and healing, this can be a strong testimony. It should not be rushed and requires careful planning. It can become a wonderful occasion for forgiveness and for teaching as to the power of a faith community to heal brokenness. It can also provide comfort and closure for the church if church disciplinary action has been followed up by the ministry of a Spiritual Care Group for the pastor and with professional counselling. This can be shared with the congregation. A Spiritual Care Group can be very helpful to a pastor. It may consist of three or four pastors who commit to meet with the pastor bi-weekly or monthly to nurture and explore with him his experience.

A Spiritual Care Group Function[256]
1. Scripture reading and prayer
2. Experiencing fellowship and support
3. Exploring issues of understanding what lead to the experience of failure
4. Seeking understanding of what one can learn from the experience
5. Encouraging ministry to the spouse and children
6. Deepening one's spiritual life
7. Assisting in finding a pathway to providing for family
8. Monitoring spiritual disciplines
9. Not rehearsing the past but creating the desired future

Figure 10.

Restoration to ministry is a complex exercise. Some are very explicit that this is not a possibility.[257] However, I do not consider this a tenable conclusion and will expand on this in the next chapter. It appears often to be motivated by a concept that the role of ministry is an elitist role that sets pastors apart from the community of faith. I find hard to reconcile this concept with my understanding of Scripture.

Others suggest a time lapse before reinstatement is considered. My approach has been to neither encourage not discourage this pursuit, but rather to explore all the ramifications of such a decision. A time lapse of at least three or four years seems appropriate, if during that time the pastor has sought and found adequate counselling, healing, restoration to their spouse, children, church community, and has re-established a disciplined Christian life.

Biblically, as we saw earlier in this book, God did not abandon broken boughs. Abraham, Elijah, David and Peter where all reinstated to ministry. The issue for Jesus in relation to Peter focused on their relationship, and that certainly seemed to be clarified in their relationship, and the coming of the Spirit at Pentecost occurred before significant ministry. Denominational guidelines differ. Certainly, the clear call of God, and the opening of doors by him, is a key. Evidence of healing, specifically in relation to contributing factors defined as related to the journey toward failure, needs to be in evidence. Restoration to one's spouse and family is basic. Full disclosure to a prospective ministry in an appropriate manner is also be important at whatever level that is deemed important. We must be carefully dependent upon the leading of the Lord in each situation.

Care and Counselling in Brokenness

The heartbeat of my approach is clearly to indicate the need for care of pastors along their entire ministry path. The Scripture quite clearly indicates God's choice and involvement in our lives.[258] Given that understanding, what happens from childhood forward is important in equipping for the ministry in which God's calling is fulfilled. If we approached the pastor's parenting, education at every level, and the development of relational skills from this perspective, it would be helpful.

However, much of the emphasis has been upon caring for pastors in the context of ministry. Each experience of ministry is different, but the need for care remains constant. The dynamic of congregations, which are volunteer groupings of people, changes the dynamic from what is experienced in most situations of non-church employment. Corporate models designed toward production or profit provides very limited help for many aspects of ministry. My experience of being a CEO in situations based upon corporate models was very different than my functioning in church communities. Pastors are often not aware of this difference, not having functioned in corporate contexts.

The stories I have shared illustrate the need for care, intervention, consultation, and counselling for people engaged in the risky environment of church communities. It is important for us to understand the relational skills and patterns of relating that provide such care. In this context, only a brief summary of what would constitute helping or caring relationships can be provided.

The Perspective from which I Speak

In the interest of complete disclosure, I want to share that my experience in this regard has been varied and has involved me in several different contexts. Pastoral ministry was my original training with a strong emphasis on evangelism. I served in chaplaincy for several years to acquired much more training in theology, psychology, trauma intervention, and clinical assessment. My certification was that of a clinical psychologist which I had opportunity to practice in a psychiatric hospital. You will understand that I have an appreciation for the effectiveness of secular therapeutic interventions.

Before you write me off, let me add that I studied theology for a dozen years as well. My passion was to integrate what I could learn from psychology with my evangelical theological perspective. It is my hope to represent the benefits of psychology with integrity as well as to represent what I consider to be a clearly Biblical approach to care and counselling for pastors and others in ministry. Much of my thinking has been shaped by engagement with many thousands of missionaries in selection, preparation, field interventions and seminars. The opportunity for involvement with many different national populations has also brought much insight.

The Central Goals of Helping Relationships

Some of the most central goals of helping relationships (whether secular or Christian) are closely integrated. Simply put, it is the goal of helping relationships to skillfully respond to the needs of people, thus enabling them to reach their chosen goals. There are significant differences between the values represented by counselling in our culture and Christian counselling. All counselling is value driven. Counselling in our culture is driven by cultural values. Christian counselling is driven by values derived from the Scriptures. A brief contrast may help.

Cultural Values	Biblical Values
• Limiting/eliminating suffering • Individual rights/respect/ dignity • Self-determination • Individual Autonomy/ independence • Right of Choice • Communal contribution	• Spiritual Relationship with God • Human dignity, worth, value of life • Eternal dimensions of mankind existence • Compassion to human need • Communal needs central to knowing man • Potential realized through God's grace • Meaning in suffering • Presence of evil

Figure 11.

One can readily see there are significant differences in the values which will express themselves in the processes that are used as well as the outcomes sought. However, it is also true that there are many similarities in the processes of helping relationships despite the contrast in value orientation. Let me illustrate this with a simple list.

Processes of Helping Relationships
• Establishing a relationship of trust and openness
• Identifying a felt need or problem to be addressed
• Creating a context for safety and confidentiality
• Exploring in an accepting environment to achieve understanding
• Clarifying values inherent in and impacting the situation
• Evaluating the process and options for achieving productive change
• Inviting accountability to assure perseverance in forward movement

Figure 12.

It is obvious that these common goals could be applied in many situations. There are additional goals that should be added from a Christian perspective. Some these will become clarified as we elaborate the process of a Biblical approach to counselling. For example, the central issues of determining and committing to God's will are paramount. In the most comprehensive definitions of counselling, there is often a distinction between the aspects of the process that facilitate exploration (empathy, respect, genuineness) and the initiative dimensions (concreteness, self-disclosure, confrontation, immediacy) which move the person toward a desired action.

From a Christian perspective, one might use Paul's definition of the responsibility of God's gifts to the church (i.e. Apostles, prophets, evangelists, pastors and teachers) *"to equip his people for works of service, so that the body of Christ may be built up until we all reach unity in the faith and in the knowledge of the Son of God and become mature, attaining to the whole measure of the fullness of in Christ."*[259] Certainly, this involves entering into a quality of relationship with another that assumes empathy, respect, and genuineness, and that will lead to concrete behavioural change. The processes for accomplishing these goals in each other's lives are clearly spelled out in the New Testament writings. Consider that the goal of bringing people to faith in Christ was not simply to achieve the certainty of heaven but to change behaviour from paganism, Jewish legalism, Greek worship, or any other to behaviour worthy of the new King and Lord of our lives.

The questions addressed by the Apostles were to discover how this was to be accomplished. There was no doubt that it began with repentance, confession, and a commitment to Christ. But that was only the beginning, and in no way, the end. To reach maturity in Christ, unity with in communities of faith, and the effective discipling of the followers of Jesus, much more was required. It is in that "much more" that we find the key to caring for each other.

I propose that we define the patterns that developed in the ministry of the Apostles and became the consistent practice and quality of the ministry of believers to each other. That ministry was the key to addressing sin, brokenness, anxiety, depression, and relational conflict in lives that needed change accomplished by the Spirit of God.

Qualities that Heal in Relationships

I will list, and briefly define, these qualities of relationship that were the expression of a transformed mind and a will captivated by a desire to serve God. These are the processes that are expressive of ministry in the New Testament. Together, they evolve into a workable definition of care and counselling from a biblical perspective. Space will not permit a detailed exegetical approach, but this will provide a start in exploring the Scriptures for our topic's understanding. In providing a definition that I believe can be sustained by Scripture, I will give only one or two references. This will facilitate any who wish to further explore the scriptural meaning of these words.

180

Love: Responding with the qualities of love, free from self-interest, with obedience and grace to all whom one would seek to care for or help.[260]

Fellowship: The actions of entering another's condition or experience in such a manner that our resources in God's grace become theirs and theirs, in turn, become ours.[261]

Edification: Relating to another person in whatever their need may be that is for their good and their resultant growth and maturity as a believer.[262]

Comfort: This describes the action of coming alongside another to bear him/her and their need lifting them that they might be strengthened and encouraged.[263]

Strengthen: The action of energizing or stimulating another by holding tightly and enduringly in support of them.[264]

Compassion: Relating to others to foster tender, compassionate, kind and sympathetic emotions toward one another.[265]

Discernment: The ability to distinguish and discriminate between choices by examining values, benefits and actions that best represent God's will.[266]

Confrontation: The action of kindly, but firmly, bringing another to awareness of the discrepancies or incongruities between their lives and their values and the will of God.[267]

These words from the Scripture adequately define the behaviour we are to relate to each other as we care and counsel each other toward maturity in Christ. These would quite adequately constitute the biblical means of caring for pastors and others in ministry in such a manner that the fruitful boughs do not break, become diseased, or enter relationships that are destructive of their ministry. We have become so accustomed to defining our responsibility in terms of evangelism that, I think, we have overlooked the quality of relationships that we are to have as believers to one another. Expressing these qualities in ministering to each other along our Christian journey, whether as pastors or lay persons, would forestall much anxiety, loneliness, sense of isolation and despair. These would foster growth and maturity. Paul speaks of this as our pursuit as the "fullness of Christ."[268]

Pastors who are carrying the burden and risks of ministry would benefit from having individuals alongside of them who could minister to them in these ways. Consider the experiences of Jim, Mel and Jordon. If each of them had fellow Christians, pastors, or mentors who had related to them during their journeys toward failure, they very likely would not have broken under the pressures they experienced. Neither the leadership of their churches, the members of their congregations, nor the leadership of their denominations intervened in the way these eight qualities of behaviour we have identified above as a Biblical response. Nor, tragically, did any of these pastors have an awareness of their need for such ministry from others.

The vulnerability that Paul so often shared of his personal life in his Epistles is often notably absent in the lives of pastors who have experience brokenness. The training of pastors prepares them to minister but does not adequately prepare them to be recipients of ministry from others. The elevation of pastors to a state above (in some manner) the members of the congregation, or to a leadership role that sets the pastor apart, or an elitism feeling of the pastoral role, or other dynamics can contribute to this state of separation. Indeed, this dynamic is found in most cases of pastoral failure.

These patterns of relationship are crucial for pastors who may have the role of shepherding or supporting other pastors in ministry. Also, denominational conferences would be best built around what is implied in these qualities of relationship. The nurture and sustenance of pastors should be a concern for denominations, churches, and pastors in their relation to each other.

Beyond Relational Care – A Theology of Weakness

It would be inappropriate to conclude this chapter without addressing three other essentials in providing care for pastors. First and foremost, we need an acute awareness of the role of the Holy Spirit of God in any attempt at prevention, intervention, or remedial care of pastors. During the journey of a pastor, who is potentially (and that includes all) heading toward the risks of brokenness, we need awareness of the ministry of the Spirit of God in both prevention and intervention. It is significant that in each of our illustrations, the pastors, quite early in their experience, began to define their experience in terms of weakness in themselves.

A theology of weakness is needed. There are six passages of Scripture from which we can derive a theology of weakness. The word translated "weakness" contains the word for strength with a prefix which gives it the meaning of "without strength." Early in their experiences, Jim, Mel and Jordon came to define their condition in addressing the variety of challenges they faced as being unable to cope. They were too weak to sustain themselves under the pressures.

First, Jesus is declared to have experienced in his incarnation the fulfillment of his desire to be one with us in temptation so that we would have a high priest who is able "to empathize with our weaknesses."[269] This clarifies the response of Jesus to our weaknesses. Indeed, the writer of Hebrews suggests that "the law appoints as high priests men in all their weakness" and, thus, conscious of their own sinfulness and need for sacrifice for sin.[270] It is very interesting that one of the qualifications of a high priest to mediate between mankind and God was that he had have awareness of their own weaknesses.

Secondly, the Holy Spirit of God responds to our weaknesses when *"we ourselves...groan inwardly...the Spirit helps us in our weaknesses...he who searches our hearts...the Spirit intercedes for God's people in accordance with the will of God."*[271] This is the response of the Holy Spirit of God to our weaknesses. The word "helps" is an interesting word. Considering all its parts, we could translate it as follows: "The Holy Spirit continuously, at his initiative, comes over against us and together with us takes a hold of our weakness." This is, indeed, the role of the Comforter whom Christ promised. Add to this the role of *the Father of compassion and the God of all comfort, who comforts us in all our troubles.*"[272] With the understanding of Jesus, the intervention of the Spirit, and the comfort of the Father, we have the resources to bring to any pastors who struggle toward brokenness.

Thirdly, the community of faith has a role to play. *"We who are strong ought to bear the failings (weaknesses) of the weak and not to please ourselves. Each of us should please his neighbors for their good, to build them up."*[273] This would apply to fellow-believers as well as fellow-pastors.

Fourthly, we must think about our own attitudes to our own weaknesses. Paul instructs us, *"I will boast of the things that show my weakness…I was given a thorn in my flesh…I plead with the Lord to take it away from me. But he said to me, 'My grace is sufficient for you, for my power is made perfect in weakness.' …Therefore…I boast all the more gladly about my weaknesses, I delight in weaknesses, in insults, in hardships, in persecutions, in difficulties. For when I am weak, then I am strong.'*[274] God is able to accomplish his purposes despite the myriad of obstructions we provide in our weaknesses. Paul boasts of two things: his weaknesses and the cross of Christ.[275]

Fifthly, in the book of Hebrews, we have a gallery of saints whom we admire in their manifestation of faith, courage, and conviction. We discover, if we study their lives, that they all had weakness. However, the writer declares that their "weakness was turned to strength."[276] Their endurance came from faith and their perseverance from the hope that faith provided.

Sixthly, we need to remind ourselves of the relationship between our weakness and God's strength. *"The weakness of God is stronger than man's strength…God chose the foolish things of the world to shame the wise; God chose the weak things of the world to shame the strong…'Let the one who boasts boast in the Lord.'"*[277] Paul writes of Christ, *"For to be sure, he was crucified in weakness, yet he lives by God's* power. *Likewise, we are weak in him, yet by God's power we will live with him in our dealing with you.*"[278] All who follow Christ in service to others need to access the strength of God through the ministry of the Holy Spirit. However, all who surround them in the community of faith have a great responsibility and opportunity to come alongside in ministry and care.

As I have walked with pastors in the remedial care, following their failure in ministry, I have discovered that we are ti be totally dependent upon the Spirit of God. One of the important aspects of that care is our dependence upon the Spirit of God to guide us in seeing God at work in those early experiences of despair and loneliness. It is important to seek the wisdom of God as to why his voice was not heard and experiencing his healing power along with the convicting power of the Spirit in revealing the sin when it is expressed in the pressure of ministry. What blinded the pastor to God's presence and the Spirit's voice? To examine these things with a view to not wasting failure, but rather learning and growing from it, contributes greatly to healing and growth. When the Psalmist spoke of God he said, *"He restores my soul."*[279] It is that restoration that we need to see daily and with courage after an experience of failure.

Caring for pastors who have broken in ministry is a case of restoring the soul. Broken boughs are souls damaged, bruised, battered, harassed, and rejected. They desperately need restoration. The Holy Spirit is the agent of that healing, but we all have a role to play as his instruments of healing and restoration.

Another essential in prevention, intervention, or healing is the role of prayer. James speaks of this very explicitly. *"Is any one of you in trouble? Let them pray...Is any among you sick? Let them call the elders of the church to pray over them and anoint them with oil in the name of the Lord. And the prayer offered in faith will make the sick person well; the Lord will raise him up. If they has sinned, they will be forgiven."*[280] Traveling with and unravelling the experience of fallen pastors requires a dependence upon prayer. The pursuit of God for wisdom is crucial.[281] Discerning what God would teach, as he brings healing to broken pastors and families, depends upon prayer and seeking God in quietness. Sometimes, just sitting quietly in an atmosphere of peace and acceptance allows the Spirit of God to speak. Learning to listen for God's voice in the pain, distrust, depression and turmoil is the most important step. Prayer is the exploration of the experience and the related issues, without judgment, so that God can speak his truth into the situation. When God speaks, it is like the creation of a great good out of the chaos of despair. Many have the illusion that pastoral counselling is speaking truth into another's situation. Often it is listening to hear the voice of God in the trauma of experience. Walking in darkness as we explore brokenness, we pray for the light of God's wisdom.

A central prayer is that of asking God to open our eyes, thus removing the scales of defensiveness, known as the timber in our own eyes, so that we may see the speck in the eye of the person in need of healing. Let me illustrate with the friends of Job. You may recall that they were most effective during the first few days when they were silent, not knowing what to say. Their presence brought more potential for healing than did their voices. When they began to speak, they spoke out of their ideas, perspectives, limitations, and, perhaps, confusion. In each case, this generated resistance, defence, and justification from Job's lips. He felt unfairly attacked and God agreed that Job's had sinned against him in their approach.

Those who would come alongside a pastor to prevent a fall or intervene when a pastor is in danger must tread carefully and prayerfully. When one is trying to bring healing to a hurting soul one must come with gentleness. It is the Spirit of God who brings conviction. Confrontation rarely does.

The burden of this book is that we will learn to provide pastors with care along their path of ministry. There are many ways that can be accomplished. My hope is to have raised some possibilities that we will all seek to implement. To use the phrase of one author, "Bring 'em back alive!"[282] The first line of defence is prevention, the second, intervention. If we work at these, the remedial work of restoration would be required less often, and God would be glorified. We would be expressing his redemptive intent as he demonstrated in relation to Abraham, David, Elijah and Peter.

Brokenness can lead to fruitfulness. As the plough breaks up the soil to render it more receptive to the seed and the harvest that follows, so brokenness in failure can render the heart more receptive to the seed of God's Word and the nurturing of the Spirit of God. Together the Word and the Spirit lead to fruitfulness. Brokenness must lead to redemptive outcomes in God's economy of Grace.

Summary:

1. Responding to the accusations of individuals in ministry leadership with caution.
2. Immediate confession and repentance are often premature and may inhibit in depth understanding.
3. Everyone impacted by the failure are in need of healing ministry.
4. Processes of restoration to fellowship and restoration to ministry must be differentiated.
5. There are central goals common to most helping relationships.
6. Biblical relationships adequately define healing patterns of ministry and restoration.

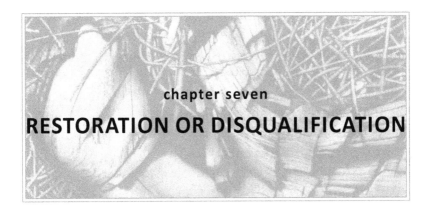

chapter seven

RESTORATION OR DISQUALIFICATION

As a reader, you may be wondering why I have not explicitly addressed the question of a moral sin and its leading to a disqualification from ministry. My reason is that the complexity of this question deserves a much lengthier discussion. In my counselling ministry with pastors, I have recommended that some disqualify themselves from ministry if it appears that there are factors in their lives that, when addressed, would lead them to that conclusion. Where that has happened, it has been clearly a conviction brought by the Holy Spirit as we have sought the wisdom of God rather than something imposed on them by human authority. Not all will be led to seek restoration to ministry. With both pastors and those desiring to engage in cross-cultural ministry, it has been helpful to take a "risk assessment" approach in determining the suitability of ministry in different contexts. If relational, spiritual, family, giftedness or any other factor such as may arise from the context of ministry are contra-indicators of evidencing jeopardy, one must question suitability for ministry. Entering inappropriate risks in ministry may have equivalency with the temptation of Jesus to leap off the high point of the temple.

I do not consider it a cop-out on my part to insist on the person seeking the call of God either to enter or to refrain from ministry. This is a decision that must, through the conviction of the Holy Spirit, be arrived at by that person and their spouse, if married. Only then can they live in peace with that decision. It is also important that re-entry to ministry be affirmed by fellow be-lievers, pastoral peers and that church leaders make their decision with knowledge. Also, if ministry requires ordination, the denom-inational leaders must be involved.

The Inconclusive Evidence of History

This is not a new problem. Scripture clearly indicates that some people were excluded from ministry, such as the sons of Eli.[283] The issue of sexual immorality among people involved in ministry was a concern to the church fathers. Jerome, Tertullian, Augustine and Francis of Assisi addressed these issues. Some individuals were accused of immorality, such as Zwingli and Henry Ward Beecher.[284] W. A. Criswell, Jerry Falwell, and Edward G. Dobson, prominent leaders of the past century, advocated dismissal from ministry for some sins.[285]

Some have accused authors of "whitewashing" the lives of reformers to enhance our honour of them by ignoring their per-sonal struggles.[286] Others declared that adulterous pastors should not be considered for restoration in ministry.[287] On the other hand, one whom I considered an excellent theologian of the past centu-ry was in favour of restoration with care.[288] Kantzer states, "The Bible does not give us a set of pat answers to these questions."[289] When we find such a mixture of opinion and experience around an issue, it seems to me we must be cautious. We need to further refine the question and the complexity of the matter being ad-dressed. I would make the following explorations in the spirit of consultation and further research of several related issues.

Ambiguity in Terminology

Having practised therapy with women heroin drug addicts, who mainly supported their habit through sexual exploitation of men and with many women who experienced a wide range of abuse from men, I may have a different perspective. Working with home-less street youth has led me to a broader perspective as to why people enter intimate relationships that meet needs, they would be unable to articulate. People frequently engage in personally harmful behaviour being driven by needs they do not understand. There is more involved than a "black or white" moral choice.

People who engage in inappropriate sexual involvement in the context of anxiety, depression, loneliness, or despair are doing so for very different reasons. Journeying with pastors, who became involved in inappropriate sexual behaviour, evidences similar variation in motivations. We must develop means of discussing sexual involvement with the awareness of the motivation that led to the engagement. This is a complex issue. However, must address deeper issues than the surface behaviour.

A major area of ambiguity in our culture arises because of the failure to clearly differentiate between the distinctive levels of sexual involvement. The term "sexual harassment" can mean anything from an uninvited look at a scantily dressed woman to aggressive rape. In a culture where sexual involvement is deemed acceptable along a wide range of behaviours, including severe abuse of partners, even with their consent, the issue becomes less clear. When sexual engagement is defined as anything from suggestive speech or accidental touch to aggressive rape, it is difficult to discuss meaningfully.

The tendency is to reduce the question to one of consent. However, there are many shades of consent. Quite frankly, in some situations involving pastors, it has been difficult to define which party was, in fact, the predator, seducer, or aggressor. Roy Bell speaks of the "bogy of the seductive woman" as a consideration.[290] Consent does not adequately address the moral failure.

Also, the literature focuses very much on the issues of the power of position, the influence of authority, the bargaining of privilege or contract, and the status differential between the partners. There appears to be an apparent expectation of entitlement. Some of these elements may be present with pastors but, in my experience, there are more common elements. One correlation I have seen would suggest a relationship between the degree of dogmatism of a pastor and his sense of power in relation to others.

In most cases, inappropriate sexual involvement followed stress, depression, anger, despair, self-incrimination, and loneliness. Often there had been a loss, for many different reasons, of intimacy with one's spouse.

Beyond Behaviour to Motivation

It may be more appropriate to think in terms of a breach of trust or a breach of integrity. The focus on sexual sins may sidetrack us from addressing the many other dimensions and expressions of sin that are a precursor to sexual expression. It becomes apparent that the motives and choices of sinful expression evidences much latitude. The reality is that some may choose pornography while another my sin in anger, bullying, fraud or harassment of others. The expressions are limitless. This shifts the focus from simply an act of behaviour toward a consideration of values and commitments. In one of his descriptive discourses about sin, Paul focuses on the internal drives to sin.[291] It becomes evident that the will to sin is motivating these individuals. Similarly, in his discussion of the unspiritual drives toward sin, he sees the drive coming from within.[292]

We need to focus our attention on sins of the heart, rather than simply focusing on behaviour. In my journey with pastors, in most cases it appeared they were driven by emotions from within. In addition to understanding their desires from a theological perspective, it is also helpful to understand the biological aspects of desire.[293]

In the illustrations provided in this book, the pastors were driven to sins of a sexual nature after their descent into depression, anger, disillusionment, despair, strong self-incrimination, and desperate loneliness. These become drivers leading to behaviours, which in their absence, would not have been chosen.

Does this remove the responsibility for sin? My answer is, "No." However, it does direct my attention to the causative factors that lead to the inappropriate and sinful behaviour. It is inadequate to simply respond to behaviour without considering "the heart" issues or the context. The wise man of Proverbs urges, "*Watch your heart with all diligence, for from it flow the springs of life.*"[294] And Jesus affirmed the same, "*But the things that come out of a person's mouth come from the heart, and these defile them.*"[295] The heart is the issue because and is the storage place to be concerned about. Scripture indicates "*evil stored up in his heart.*"[296] I would refer you back to the section dealing with "The Inner Nature of Sin."

When dealing with broken pastors, church leadership will often get into major conflictual situations when they focus only on the guilt or innocence based on behaviour. The judging of behaviour, without understanding of the motivations or the contributing factors leading to the behaviour, most frequently elicits a negative reaction, if not a denial. This is not to overlook the behaviour but to understand it and minister to the foundational motivations. This is illustrated in Nathan's confrontation of David.

The Body as Sacred

A primary issue in any form of abuse is a failure to recognize that we get our understanding of the human being by seeing the value God places on the body. In our culture there is no understanding of the body and its relationship to the whole person, and especially sexuality, as Paul understood it. In his lengthy discussion of sexual immorality, Paul is very explicit.[297] He contrasts what is permissible and what is beneficial. The body is for the Lord and is a member of Christ. Uniting one's body to another is becoming one with the other as we are one with the Lord. He, then, declares that sexual sins are sins against one's own body, which is a temple of the Holy Spirit. "*Therefore honor God with your bodies.*"[298] Sexual sin is not just inappropriate behaviour but rather it is soul-destroying actions that come from desires within. One must be careful in speaking of sexual behaviour that has become addictive in the same manner as other addictive behaviour. The Biblical view of sexuality is quite different engaging the whole person. It is much more than behaviour. The desire that leads to sexual misconduct is much more than a disease and is a deeper problem than many other behaviours.

A theology of the body would provide considerable restraint to inappropriate sexual engagement.[299] It is also clear that, if we understood God's perspective of our bodies, we would be less likely to abuse ourselves in the way that Jim, Mel, and Jordon did so in ministry. Earlier in the book, we identified the processes which led to sin in the life of these men. These men, from one perspective, abused themselves in over-extension, lack of care, and loss of nurturing relationships. They expressed that by retreating from health-inducing relationships. A high Christian view of the body accentuates the magnitude of sexual sin. Also, our inability to openly and explicitly deal with sexual concerns gives that human reality much more power over us than it deserves.

Restoration or No Restoration

It is my position that the complexity of the issue of restoration is profound. It requires a full understanding of the failure and the restoration to a relationship with spouse, family, church, denomination, and others. God's dealing with man, beginning with the Fall of Adam and Eve, has been all about restoration and redemption. We await the restoration and renewal of all things in a New Heaven and New Earth. It is appropriate to practise forgiveness and restoration in response to repentance and forgiveness within our church communities today. The percentage of churches who seek restoration to fellowship is relatively small. It is easier to get a new pastor than to restore one, even to fellowship. This hard work requiring the deep commitment Christ expects of us. There are several issues that require a closer examination, if we are to understand the issues related to the restoration to ministry. We should be clear that the restoration to God, family, church, and others is a very different question than restoration to ministry.

The authors of the article, *"Why Adulterous Pastors Should Not be Restored,"*[300] reference Kenneth Kantzer in their introduction as saying, "Genuine forgiveness does not necessarily imply restoration to leadership." However, in an article in the same magazine, *"The Road to Restoration,"*[301] Kenneth Kantzer discusses the road to restoration. He writes, "These guidelines, drawn generally from Holy Scripture, are not a rigid and invariable formula." This much more accurately represents the Kantzer whom I read.

As I study the argument, it seems to me that we must clarify the pathway to repentance, confession, and forgiveness from Scripture. Another issue we would do well to study is the way sin is confronted in Scripture. Unfortunately, the model of Nathan, Jesus, and God in responding to sin is often not displayed in responding to pastors who fail. It seems to me that it is inadequate to simply define pastoral adultery as "an even greater sin."[302] Nor is it adequate to expound the nature of sexual sin since there is no question where the Scripture stands on that question. The argument from the perspective of pastoral qualification to be blameless, as important as all the qualifications are, does not adequately address the problem. No one would wish to minimize the requirement of discipline and restraint. These are urged consistently in Scripture.

The question of the higher standard and thus the judgment of pastors must be done in the light of several passages of Scripture.[303] James speaks of the teacher being "judged more strictly." Paul clearly outlines the care that must be taken in selecting leadership. He also gives his response to those who sought to judge his ministry. A full study of the question of judgment and its differentiation from discernment is helpful. Discernment is a function of comparative analysis whereas judgment is a forensic term used in reference to the determination of a judge in a court of law. The verb, as in James, may have more to do with the care in selection or desire for ministry that it references judgment in response to sin. Paul urges caution in accusing pastors. These perspectives would benefit from the clarity that may come from scholarly study.

I would explore the possibility that an implication behind much of the argument comes from an understanding of the pastor as being apart from the common Christian. It may be related to concepts of leadership that place the leader above his congregation as more morally responsible or being closer to God and, therefore, required to be separate from the temptations and taint of sin. This places the pastor more in a role of "priest" or "king," to use the Old Testament terminology. I do not see that in the New Testament. In Paul's discussion of the church as a body[304], it is interesting that before discussing those with specialized roles in the body (who are, indeed, gifts appointed by God), Paul expounds the function of the members of the body in terms of the ministry that is to occur toward each other. The picture I get from the New Testament is of the leadership being among, with or within the flock rather than above, over, or having some priestly function that sets them apart from the community of faith.

It is important to acknowledge that some authors would not accept my suggestion that the examples of God's response to Abraham, Elijah, and David, or that of Jesus to Peter, are valid.[305] It seems that this objection arises from defining the "pastoral" role as significantly different than that of the heroes of the faith. I would observe that these men are presented as models and that God's response to them, or to others, is an expression of his grace to all who serve him out of the "weaknesses" of human fallenness.[306] If the response of Jesus to Peter does not provide us with an example of his compassion and wisdom in dealing with us, I think we are at a profound disadvantage in knowing how God responds to us in our function as clay vessels bearing the gifts of God. Being the bearers of God's grace to others requires us to have an assurance of God's grace in our failings.

Some who have shared with me their anger, disappointment, and, yes, even their desire for revenge toward a fallen pastor seem to be trying hard to defend the purity, holiness of God, or the justice of God in judgement against sin. I don't think God's character needs or benefits from that defence. More frequently, it appears to me that these expressions arise from a need within the person, or as an outburst of hurt, disappointment or anger. Nor does such an approach follow the example of Jesus in his relationship to sinners so abundantly illustrated in his life.

The path toward restoration to ministry is arduous and, in my experience, rather long. It takes much courage, vulnerability, and a pursuit of God's grace. However, if that path is trod over some adequate time period and, if God calls a person to restoration to ministry, I would fear to stand in the way. My role is to journey with that person redemptively to reconciliation and a restorative desire of God for their lives. Claiming the right of a judge inhibits that function.

It is my prayer that we might seek an understanding of moral sin or any other kind of failure, work hard to redeem the fallen, and pray much for the wisdom and ministry of the Spirit of God in finding his will into the future. That future is in his hands and I am content to leave it there.

Summary:

1. There are a variety of perspectives about Restoration and the timing.
2. Ambiguity about defining sexuality creates much confusion, misunderstanding and minimizing of moral issues.
3. We must go deeper than behaviour to understand the nature of sin, as Jesus did.
4. Further discussion is necessary with a strong focus on the redemptive grace of God.

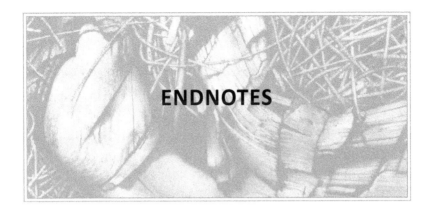

ENDNOTES

1   Leviticus 19
2   Leviticus 19:23
3   Psalm 1:3
4   Jeremiah 17:7 - 8
5   Luke 6:43 - 45
6   James 5:17
7   2 Corinthians 4:7

Chapter One – Biblical Fruitful Boughs Broken
8   Isaiah 51:2
9   Isaiah 41:8
10   2 Chronicles 20:7
11   James 2:23
12   James 2:22
13   Genesis 12:1
14   Hebrews 11:8
15   Acts 7:2
16   Isaiah 51:2
17   Genesis 12:7
18   Genesis 13:10
19   Genesis 14:2
20   Genesis 12:8
21   Genesis 13:4
22   Genesis 13:14; 14:22

23 Hebrews 11:10
24 Genesis 15:1
25 Genesis 13:15
26 Genesis 17:3 - 8
27 Genesis 14:18 - 26
28 Genesis 17:1
29 Genesis 21:33
30 Genesis 22:14
31 1 Corinthians 10:13; 1 Peter 1:7; James 1:12
32 Genesis 22
33 Hebrews 11:19
34 Genesis 22:5
35 Genesis 22:4 - 8
36 Genesis 22:14
37 Genesis 22:18
38 Genesis 12:10
39 Genesis 12:12
40 Genesis 12:13
41 Genesis 12:10
42 Genesis 20
43 Genesis 20:4 - 7
44 Genesis 16
45 Genesis 16:2
46 Genesis 16:5
47 Genesis 16:13
48 2 Samuel 23:1
49 See 1 Samuel, 2 Samuel and 1 Kings
50 1 Samuel 16:3,7
51 1 Samuel 16:13
52 Matthew 1:1, 12:23, 15:22, 21:9; Romans 1:1 - 3. See many
    other references in the Gospels. Revelation 5:5
53 2 Samuel 7:12:16
54 1 Samuel 17
55 1 Samuel 18:8
56 1 Samuel 24

57 1 Samuel 20:23 - 25
58 Psalm 40:1
59 1 Samuel 30:23 - 25
60 See 1 Samuel 25
61 2 Samuel 7
62 2 Samuel 8:14
63 2 Samuel 5:10
64 2 Samuel 7:20 - 22
65 F.B. Meyer, David: Shepherd, Psalmist, King, (London: Morgan and Scott, no date), pg. 172
66 2 Samuel 11
67 Job 31:1
68 2 Samuel 12
69 2 Samuel 12:13
70 See Psalm 51, 55, 41
71 2 Samuel 12:14
72 2 Samuel 12:13
73 2 Samuel 23, 24
74 1 Chronicles 28:9, 20
75 Malachi 4:5
76 Matthew 11:14
77 Matthew 17
78 James 5:17 - 18
79 1 Kings 17:1
80 1 Kings 18:46
81 1 Kings 19
82 1 Kings 19:3
83 1 Kings 19:7
84 I Kings 19:9
85 See in a later chapter Personal Indicators of Stress
86 1 Kings 19:11
87 2 Kings 1:1 - 18
88 2 Kings 1:16 - 17
89 2 Kings 2:11 - 12
90 Micah 4:5

91 John 1:35
92 John 1:38 - 39
93 Matthew 16:18
94 Luke 5:8 - 10
95 Matthew 4:19
96 Mark 1:29 - 37
97 Luke 9:35
98 Matthew 14
99 Matthew 16:16
100 John 13
101 Luke 22:45,46
102 Luke 22:31 - 32
103 Luke 22:46
104 Luke 22:51
105 Luke 33:53
106 John 21:15 - 23
107 I Corinthians 1:12, 3:4 - 6, 22
108 1 Corinthians 4:7
109 1 Corinthians 4:1 - 5
110 If the experience of transition interests you, you might want
to see my book, *"Pastoral Transitions"* or similar literature. We
studied along with others on a research team the experience
of hundreds of individuals who experienced cross-cultural
engagement.
111 F.B. Myer, David, Shepherd, Psalmist, King, (London: Morgan and Scott.) p. 172
112 2 Corinthians 11:16 - 29

Chapter Two – Modern Fruitful Boughs Broken
113 2 Corinthians 5:12
114 John 21:3
115 See the Biblical stories: Judges 3:12; 1 Samuel 8:5
116 G.K. Chesterton, *Heretics*, (1905) p. 9 (www.gutenberg.org/
files/470/470-h/470-h.htm)

117 Matthew 13

118 1 Corinthians 4:4

119 Psalm 73

120 Galatians 5:16 - 24

121 Romans 13:9

122 Galatians 5:16 - 18

123 1 John 2:16 Some older translations used the words, "bowels of compassion"

124 Matthew 9:36, Luke 7:13; 10:33; 15:20

125 1 John 3:17

126 Revelation12:10, 1 Peter 5:8, Matthew 4:3, 1 Peter 1:9

127 Matthew 12:24, John 14:30, 12:31, 16:11, Ephesians 6:12, Ephesians 2:2, 2 Corinthians 4:4

128 John 8:4, Matthew 13:19, Genesis 3;4, John 8:4

129 Genesis 3:5

130 Romans 7

131 C. S. Lewis. *The Screwtape Letters and The Abolition of Man*, (United Kingdom: William Collins Sons, 1942, 1043)

132 2 Thessalonians 2:12

133 Job 1 throughout the book

134 Psalm 38:11

135 Matthew 13:25

136 2 Chronicles 21

137 2 Corinthians 2:11

138 2 Corinthians 11:3 - 15

139 1 Thessalonians 3:5

140 Luke 22:31

141 Matthew 4; Luke 4; Hebrews 2:18, 4:15

142 Judges 6:36

143 2 Corinthians 12:7

144 Matthew 26:67, Mark 14:65, 1 Corinthians 4:11, 1 Peter 2:20

145 Romans 16:20

146 Hebrews 2:14; Revelation 20

147 Luke 22:32

148 1 John 2:1

149 James 4:7
150 2 Corinthians 12:8
151 Hebrews 11:34
152 See 1 Corinthians 10:13; Hebrews 2:14; Revelation 12:11

Chapter Three – Comparing Contributing Factors

153 Jonah 4:1 - 11
154 John 21:15 - 23
155 2 Corinthians 10:7
156 The Biblical pictures in Christ's parables from nature and the agrarian nurture necessary to fruitfulness is helpful to consider.
157
158 One of the early studies of this, privately published, was William L. White. Incest in the Organizational Family: the ecology of burnout in closed systems, (IL: Lighthouse Training Institute, 1986)
159 Zechariah 3:1
160 Ephesians 6:10-18; 2 Corinthians 12:7
161 1 John 3:8
162 Romans 3:9; 5:12-13; 7:1-8:13
163 Romans 6:6
164 For a detailed discussion see Nancy R. Pearcey, Love Thy Body, (MI: Baker Publishing, 2018), chapter 7.
165 1 Corinthians 12:12ff; Ephesians 4:1-7
166 Matthew 18:1-14; Mark 9:42; Romans 9:32f
167 Romans 14; 1 John 2:10; Leviticus 19:14
168 Romans 16:17
169 Matthew 13:36ff
170 1 Corinthians 4:1-5
171 1 Corinthians 5:1-12
172 2 Corinthians 2:5-11
173 Matthew 16:13; Ephesians 2:20, 4:15; Colossians 1:18; Acts 20:28; 2 Corinthians 11:2; Revelation 12:2; John 1:12; Romans 8:15; Philippians 2:15; 1 John 3:1
174 Ephesians 3:9-11

175 Ephesians 4 & 2; 1 Corinthians 3:9
176 Romans 12:1-6; Romans 15:1-2; 1 Corinthians 13; Galatians 6:1-5
177 Galatians 6:1-5
178 1 Corinthians 14:22-32
179 Colossians 3:1-17
180 1 Thessalonians 4:1-12
181 1 Timothy 1:3-7,19-20; 6:4f; 2:14-19, 22-24; 4:10
182 Titus 1:5, 10-14; 3:9-11
183 1 Corinthians 1:10-13; 3:1-4; 6:1-8, 12-20; 8:12
184 Galatians 1:6; 5:13-15
185 Revelation 2:1-3:21
186 2 Corinthians 11:28
187 1 Thessalonians 3:10
188 2 Corinthians 1:8f
189 2 Corinthians 7:5-6
190 1 Corinthians 7:1-7
191 This is evidence by the collection of money to relieve the poverty of the church in Jerusalem. 1 Corinthians 16
192 1 Thessalonians 2:1-12
193 1 Corinthians 7
194 There is much discussion over the data re pastors leaving the ministry. Some will suggest 1500 or more per month in North America while others suggest 500 may be more accurate. The number of pastors I have engaged convince me that is too many. Check the literature references, if this is of interest to you.

Chapter Four – The Journeys Toward Failure

195 See research of Robert Huizinga, "Broken Faith: What happens When a Church Decides to Lay-off a Pastor" (Apr. 2018, Doctoral Thesis, Regent College).
196 For further study one might consult, Bessel Van Der Kolk, The Body Keeps the Score, (UK: Random House, Penguin,

2014) . Dr. Kolk is considered a foremost authority. See Biography for other references.

197. See for a discussion of anger: Glenn Taylor and Rod Wilson, *Helping Angry People* (Vancouver, British Columbia: Regent Publishing, 1977) and Glenn Taylor and Rod Wilson, *Exploring Your Anger* (Vancouver, British Columbia: Regent Publishing 1977)

198 William Shakespeare, *Macbeth*, Act 2, Scene 3, page 4 (https://www.sparknotes.com p. 68)

199 From Glenn C. Taylor. Pastors in Transition: Navigating the Turbulence of Change (MB: Word Alive Press, 2013) p.14.

200 Bessel Van Der Kolk, *The Body Keeps Score*. (United Kingdom: Random House, Penguin, 2014)

201 Genesis 3

202 Genesis 12, 16 and 18

203 Job 2

204 Hosea 1:2

205 1 Corinthians 7 and 9

Chapter Five – Preventions and Interventions

206 Ephesians 2:9; 3:6

207 See Romans 16:7; 2 Corinthians 8:23; 1 Thessalonians 3:2; Philippians 2:25; 4:3; Colossians 1:7; 4:7, 10, 11; and Philemon 2:23.

208 2 Corinthians 7:5 - 7

209 Genesis 26:2 - 3

210 James 5:7

211 1 Kings19:21

212 2 Kings 1:10 - 12

213 James 5:17

214 See Chapter 4:3

215 Jeremiah 1:4 - 10

216 Psalm 139:14 - 16

217 Hebrew 11:34

218 Acts 13:1 - 3

219 1 Samuel 3:1 - 21

220 The words for slave, deacon and stewardship describe some of these. Others are found in secular literature.

221 Much research has yielded varying statistics. These may be explored in works by the following authors: Barna Group; Burns; Carroll, Elkington, Graham and fellow authors; Lewis Center for Church Growth; LifeWay; MacKenzie; Merrill; Trinity Western University and Wilson (2015). See the Bibliography.

222 2 Corinthians 7:2 - 7; 13 - 16

223 Acts 23:11

224 Acts 27:23

225 Exodus 18:17

226 1 Timothy 5:17 - 20

227 Hebrews 13:7

228 1 Thessalonians 5:12 - 13

229 Philemon 2:12

230 Philippians 2:29

231 John 16:33

232 Matthew 24:9

233 2 Corinthians 12:7

234 2 Corinthians 11:28

235 2 Corinthians 7:5

236 1 Corinthians 4:3

237 2 Corinthians 4:6 - 12

238 I would call this "Positional Leadership." This is not the place to expand this but let me suggest it involved strong emphasis on the integrity, unity, complementarity, trust and integrity of each contributing member of the body.

239 For example: there slaves who were in bondage, attendants of children, servants in charge (officers), attendants to health needs, and stewards of households.

240 1 Samuel 2

241 For a discussion of anger in church ministry see: Glenn Taylor and Rod Wilson, *Helping Angry People* and *Exploring your Anger*, (Vancouver, British Columbia: Regent Publishing, 1977)

242 Job 30: 27, 11

243 T.S. Eliot, *The Cocktail Party*, (free download as PDF: https//www.scribd.com/doc, March 2019)

244 Mathew Arnold, *The Buried Life*, (https://www.poetryfoundation.org:poems, March 2019)

Chapter Six – Responding to Broken Boughs

245 Matthew 18:15 - 19

246 Galatians 6:1 - 4; James 5:13 - 16

247 1 Timothy 5:19

248 Psalm 51:4

249 James 5:16 - 20 (The Message)

250 Romans 2:1 - 4

251 Ephesians 2:7

252 Zechariah 12:10; Romans 7; Psalm 51; Numbers 23:34; Joshua 7:9

253 Roman 7

254 Psalm 142:7

255 Galatians 6:1 - 5; James 5:19 - 20

256 See Galatians 1:18; 2:1 - 10; Acts 18:21; 21:17 - 20

257 See Kent Hughes and John Armstrong, "Why adulterous Pastors should not be Restored," Christianity Today, (Carol Stream: Illinois), April 3, 1995.

258 Ephesians 1:4,11; Jeremiah 1:4 - 12

259 Ephesians 4:9 - 13

260 1 John 2:3 - 12; 1 Corinthians 13:1 - 13. Related words are cleave, endure with.

261 This word may the least understood word in the New Testament. It is used of sharing gifts, food, material goods, money, participation, partnership and resources. It reached across racial, cultural boundaries and describes both our participation in Christ's redemptive work and our engagement in each other's lives. Romans 15:26; Ephesians 3:1 - 12; Galatians 2:6 - 10

262 1 Corinthians 14:5, 12, 26

263 2 Corinthians 1:3 - 7; Romans 15:10; Galatians 6:2

264 Romans 1:11; Acts 16:5; 1 Thessalonians 5:14

265 1 Thessalonians 5:14; Hebrews 4:15, 10:34; Romans 12:9 - 10

266 Acts 17:11; 1 Corinthians 2:14. This word is to be differentiated from judgment.

267 1 Corinthians 10:11; Ephesians 6:4; Titus 3:10; Romans
15:14; Colossians 3:16

268 Ephesians 4:13

269 Hebrew 2:9, 4:15

270 Hebrews 7:28

271 Romans 8:22 - 27

272 2 Corinthians 1:3 - 7

273 Romans 15:1 - 2

274 2 Corinthians 11:30 - 12:10

275 Galatians 6:4

276 Hebrews 11 (see verse 12); Hebrews 12:2,7,11

277 1 Corinthians 1:25 - 31

278 2 Corinthians 13:3 - 4

279 Psalm 23:3

280 James 5:13 - 16

281 James 1:5; Colossians 1:9

282 Dave Burchett. *Bring 'em Back Alive,* (New York: Random
House, 2004)

Chapter Seven – Restoration or Disqualification

283 1 Samuel 2:22

284 Roy Bell, "Power and Loss of Integrity" in *Why Christian
Leaders Fall.* (Langley:) British Columbia: Trinity Western
University Symposium March 1996). Page 3-4

285 Paul Bramer. "Let Him Who Thinks He Stands Take Heed":
Sexual Immorality in Male Christian Leadership. (Personally, prepared and presented research paper, 1990)

286 Scott Hubbard. "Whitewashed Heroes, The Flaws in our Reformers." Desiring God, https//www.desiringgod.org, (Oc-
tober 26, 2011).

287 R. Kent Hughes and John H. Armstrong. "Why Adulterous Pastors Should not be Restored." Christianity Today (Carol Stream: Illinois, April 3, 1995).

288 Kenneth Kantzer. "The Road to Restoration." Christianity Today (Carol Stream, Illinois, November 20, 1987)

289 Ibid, page 2.

290 Bell, op cit., page 4.

291 2 Timothy 3:1 - 9

292 Romans 7:7 - 25

293 See Marc Lewis. *The Biology of Desire: Why Addiction is not a Disease.* (Toronto, Canada, 2015)

294 Proverbs 4:23

295 Matthew 15:18

296 Luke 6:45

297 1 Corinthians 6:12 - 20

298 1 Corinthians 6:20

299 A helpful study of this area is provided by: Nancy Pearcey, *Love Thy Body: Answering Hard Questions About Life and Sexuality.* (Grand Rapids, Michigan, Baker Books, 2018)

300 R. Kent Huges and John H. Armstrong, op cit., April 3, 1995.

301 Kenneth Kantzer, op cit., November 20, 1987.

302 See R. Kent Hughes and John Armstrong, op cit., April 3, 1995.

303 James 3:1; 1 Timothy 3; 1 Corinthians 4:1 - 5

304 1 Corinthians 12:12 - 31

305 Ibid, page 2.

306 Hebrews 11:34

EPILOGUE

For anyone who has experienced betrayal, humiliation, shunning or emotional breakdown in any group or community context will know, as I do, the excruciating and traumatic impact of these experiences. Regardless of issues of personal responsibility, moral failure, or any other kind of cumulative weakness, the Christian community's response often bears no resemblance to the clear heart of mercy, repair and longing for restoration that Scripture demonstrates in both Testaments. The model of Jesus illustrates God's intent.

Anyone involved in team or organizational leadership in Christian community, sooner of later has to deal with imperfection, roadblocks, collapse of relationships and sometimes the collapse of individuals we count on. For this reason, leadership, like the journey laid out in this book is not for the faint of heart. It is a journey into vulnerability, shared responsibility, trail and error and yes, recognition of all of our own limitations and errors in judgment. Thank God, we have all also experienced grace and reconciliation with Him.

I celebrate this powerful contribution to an essential toolbox written by Glenn, of pastoral oversight, with a pastor's heart. I offer these complimentary reflections in poetry and cover art, a calk work, *Lazarus*, in the hope that men and women in ministry can help raise up soldiers instead of burying them alive.

—James Tughan

BIBLIOGRAPHY

Jovan Barrington, "When a Church Breaks Up with You," Patheos, (www.patheos.com/blogs/jesuscreed/006/01/27/)

Barna Group, *Burnout & Breakdowns: Barna's Risk Metric for Pastors.* (California: Barna Group, 2017)

Paul Bramer, *"Let him who thinks he stands take heed: sexual immorality in male Christian Leadership."* Discussion paper presented to pastors, 1990.

Walter Brueggemann, *The Psalms & the Life of Faith (ed. P.D. Miller).* (MN: Fortress, 1995)

Dave Burchet, *Bring 'Em Back Alive.* (Colorado: Waterbrook Press, 2004)

Bob Burns, Tasha Chapman & Donald Guthrie, *Resilient Ministry.* (Illinois: InterVarsity, 2013)

Ray Carrol, *Fallen Pastor: Finding Restoration in a Broken Word.* (Calfiornia: Civitas Press, 2011)

Henry Cloud, *Necessary Endings,* (New York: HarperCollins, 2010)

Joe Crider, *Confessions of a fallen Worship Pastor.* (Kentucky:Southern Equip, April 9, 2017)

Robert Elkington, *Adversity in Pastoral Leadership.* (Canada: Verbatum et Ecclesia 34(1), Art. #821, http://dx.doi.org/10.4102/ve.v34i1.821, August, 2013)

Richard Exley, *Perils of Power: Immorality in the Ministry.* (Oklamoma: Honor Books, 1988)

Thomas Graham, Jan Sattem, Richard Moline, *Regarding the Matter of Fallen Leaders within the Free Church and their Restoration.* (Study paper, March, 1990)

R. Kent Hughes, & John H. Armstrong, *"Why Adulterous Pastors Should Not be Restored"* Christianity Today,(Illinois: April 3, 1995)

Robert Huizinga, *"Broken Faith: What Happens When a Church Decides to Lay-off a Pastor,P"* (Virginia: Regent University, Ph.D. Thesis, April, 2018)

Gary Inrig, *Forgiveness* (Michiagan: Discovery House, 2005.)

Jeff Iorg, *The Painful Side of Leadership.* (Twennasee: B& H Publishing, 2009)

Don Jeffries, *No Fall Too Far* (Arizona: August House, 1992)

David Jeremiah, *Learning to Live by Faith.* (California: Turning Point, 2003)

Kenneth Kantzer, *"The Road to Restoration."* (Illinois: Christianity Today, November 20, 1987)

R. T. Kendall, *Total Forgiveness.* (Florida: Charisma House, 2002)

Chuck Lawless, *Explanations/Confessions of Pastors who Fell.* www.chuchlawless.com/, April 28, 2017.

James Lawrence, *Growing Leaders: Cultivating Discipleshiip for Yourself and Others.* (United Kingdom: CPAS, 2004)

Lewis Center for Church Growth (Eds. Weems,Jr, Lovett & Arnold, Joseph). *Clergy Health: A review of literature.* (Illinois: Lewis Centre for Health, January, 2009)

Marc Lewis, *The Biology of Desire: Why Addiction is not a Disease.* (Canada: Doubleday, 2015)

Life Way, *Pastors are not Quitting in Droves.* (Tennessee: Lifeway, September 28, 2016.)

Gordon MacDonald, *Mid-Course Correction.* (Tennessee: Thomas Nelson, 2000)

Mike MacKenzie, *Why Moral Failure Happens When Ministry is Going Great.* (Illinois: CTPastors, June, 2017)

Gabor Mate, *When the Body Says No: The Hidden Cost of Stress.* (Canada: Vintage, 2012)

Herbert Martin, *Are you listening, former Pastor?* (Maryland: Ministry, March, 1993)

Dean Merrill, *Clergy Couples in Crisis.* (Texas: Word Books, 1985)

Peter Mosgofian, & George Ohlschlager, *Sexual Misconduct in Counseling and Ministry.* (Illinois: Word, 1995)

Name Withheld, *When a Pastoral Colleague Falls,* (Illinios: Leadership, Winter Quarter, 1991)

Robert Peach, *"Please Get Help."* (Maryland: Ministry, May, 1992)

Nancy R. Pearcey, *Love Thy Body: Answering Har Questions About Life and Sexuality.* (Michigan: Baker Books, 2018)

Claude Pratte, *Guidelines for Pastors to Deal Successfully with Temptation to Sexual Sin,* (Texas: Dallas Theological Seminary, M.Th. Thesis, 1984)

Frauke Schaefer, & Charles Schaefer, *Tauma & Resilience: Effectively Supporting those who Serve God.* (California: Condeo Press, 2012)

Tim Stafford, *As Our Years Increase.* (Minnesota: Zondervan, 1989)

Lyle Schaller, *The InterVentionist.* (Tennessee: Abingdon Press, 1997)

Donald P. Smith, *Clergy in the Cross Fire.* (Philadelphia: Westminster Press, 1972)

Melvin Steinbron, *Can the Pastor Do it Alone.* (California: Regal, 1987)

Richard Stenbakken, *The Affair,* (MD: Ministry, March, 1993)

Charles Stanley, *Emotional Baggage in the Ministry,* (Virginia: Christian Counseling Today, January, 1993)

Richard Tedeschi, & Lawrence G. Calhoun, *Trauma & Transformation.* (United Kingdom: Sage, 1995)

Glenn C. Taylor, *Pastors in Transition: Navigating the Turbulence of Change.* (Winnipeg, MB: Word Alive Press, 2013)

Glenn C. Taylor, *The Web of Life: An Invitation to Life or to Die in the Fabric of Community.* (Winnipeg, MB: Word Alive Press, 2016)

Glenn Taylor, & Rod Wilson, *Helping Angry People.* (Vancoucer, BC: Regent College, 1997)

Glenn Taylor, & Rod Wilson, *Exploring Your Anger.* (Vancouver, BC: Regent College, 1997)

Trinity Western University, *Why Christian Leaders Fall.* (Vancouver, BC. Trinity Western University Symposium, 1996)

Paul David Tripp, *Dangerous Callling.* (Illinois: Crossway, 2012)

Bessel Van Der Kolk, *The Body Keeps the Score.* (United Kingdom: Random House, Penguin, 2014)

Jeff VanVonderen, *Tired of Trying to Measure Up.* (Minnesota: Bethany, 1989)

Miroslav Volf, *Exclusion and Embrace.* (Tennessee: Abingdon, 1996)

Michael Walker, *The God of Our Journey.* (United Kingdom: Marshall Morgan & Scott, 1989)

Earl & Sandy Wilson, & Paul & Virginia Friesen, & Larry & Nancy Paulson, Larry, *Restoring the Fallen: A Team Approach to Caring, Confronting & Reconciling.* (Illinois: InterVarsity, 1997)

Ear; Wilson, *Steering Clear: Avoiding the Slippery Slope of Moral Failure.* (Illinios: InterVarsity, 2002)

Michael Wilson, & Brad Hoffman, *Preventing Ministry Failure.* (Illinios: InterVarsity Press, 2007)

Michael T. Wilson, *Unburdened: The Christian Leader's Path to Sexual Integrity.* (Illinios: InterVarsity, 2015)

ABOUT THE AUTHOR

It has been helpful to me to have summary information about authors I read. It provides a context into which I can place what they are discussing. Since this summary covers eight decades, it will hit only the highlights that provide a context for this book.

My faith journey began as a teenager. My excitement in hearing the Gospel for the first time started me on a great adventure in faith and life. I was the first in my family of six siblings to have the opportunity to go to secondary school. My motivation for seeking Seminary training was to acquire Biblical knowledge to teach a class of nine-year-old boys in Sunday school. While attending Seminary, I engaged in pioneering churches and married. Over a period of seven years we started three churches. Three frustrations developed: I felt ill-equipped to disciple individuals, to deal with church tensions and depression induced by over-extension and inadequate salary. Further education seemed the best answer. This was made possible by working in Correctional services while completing graduate degrees in psychology and theology.

My next transition was into Bible College and Seminary teaching and counseling students. The last three years of this twelve-year period was as Assistant to the President. For almost eight years following I served as General Director of a large inner-city ministry, Yonge Street Mission, in Toronto, and eighteen years as Director of Counselling Services at Missionary Health

Institute and International Health Management brought me to retirement in 2005.

During the years since 1970, I also served as president of our Baptist denomination, served on an international mission board, provided psychological assessments, orientation programs and debriefing for several thousand missionaries (from over 25 different mission organizations) and visited over twenty countries providing training, consulting and conflict-management services for both missionaries and nationals. Many on-field training seminars for missionary leaders and nationals were conducted. A very fulfilling experience for me was participation in the development of a mobile member care team (www.mmct.org) which functioned different locations around the world.

Providing counselling, consultation and conflict resolution for churches and pastors during these years was a major involvement. My wife and I provided a retreat centre for missionaries, their children and pastoral families for eleven years. During that time over 1600 people in ministry came to our home for one to fourteen days for retreat and counseling.

A major influence on me was the opportunity to be involved with seven other professionals who provided research for a dozen mission organizations to study the issues surrounding the boarding school experience of children, transition experiences for families and the contributors to family success in missions. Participation and leadership in international conferences addressing concerns of those involved in ministry broadened my perspective.

In retirement, I continue to consult with churches of several denominations and to walk with pastors through difficulties. The opportunities have very expensive both with pastors and denominational leaders. The variety of situations encountered in this ministry has led to the convictions expressed in this book.